CAMERA GIRL

Mirror Books

Published by Mirror Books,
an imprint of Trinity Mirror plc,
1 Canada Square,
London E14 5AP, England

www.mirrorbooks.co.uk
twitter.com/themirrorbooks

Executive Editor: Jo Sollis
Editor: Robin Jarossi
Art Director: Julie Adams
Photoshop and Image Production: Paul Mason

ISBN 9781910335475

First hardback edition

Printed and bound in Great Britain
by CPI Group (UK) Ltd, Croydon, CR0 4YY

Contents

*This book is dedicated to my family:
past, present and future…*

'Two Tarts'

I'm squashed in the doorway of the ladies' loo in a London pub. It's not at all a ladylike position to be in. Maybe I should be asking myself what the bloody hell I'm doing here, but I don't have time for that now.

I'm peeking out at two young girls a few yards away. They're having a drink, their long legs folded underneath one of those small tables, talking in intimate whispers to each other. One is a tall, leggy creature with sad eyes; the other a pert little blonde. They're lost in deep conversation. They could be any two girls from the streets of Swinging London; shop assistants, hairdressers, shorthand typists. But, apart from the Queen herself, they're currently the two most famous women in the country, at the eye of a storm that's rocking the nation. In years to come, it will even be said that they brought down the government. The year is 1963. The girls are Christine Keeler and Mandy Rice-Davies.

It's the first day of the Stephen Ward trial at the Old Bailey, just along the road. Newspapers like mine are calling it, as usual, the trial of the century but this time they're probably right.

When the tip-off flashes into the office, all the *Daily Mirror*'s team of photographers are out on other jobs. All except me.

'Those two tarts are in the Long Bar in Holborn,' the message says. 'Better move fast.'

Those two tarts. Not very nice. Christine and Mandy aren't themselves on trial, but the media and the public have already judged them. Even in these supposedly liberated times, the old attitudes to women still cling like barnacles.

When the reporter and I reach the Long Bar, it turns out the tip-off was far from exclusive. Outside, there's a grumpy knot of pressmen who've already been kicked out by an even grumpier landlord. But my reporter and I sail right in, like any young couple nipping in for a quick one at lunchtime. Who'd ever imagine a woman might be a photographer on a national newspaper? A woman might be a tart or a monarch, but a press photographer? Pull the other one.

The bar is dark, the lighting awful, the air foggy with cigarette smoke. It won't be easy. Then I spot the loo. I leave my reporter buying the drinks. With my camera under my coat and my heart in my mouth, I slip inside the toilet then wedge the door open with my foot, the crack just wide enough. I haven't got a flash but I work out the exposure and adjust the camera.

A photographer I respect always says it's easy to take photos but so much harder to get a 'picture'. An image that somehow captures the essence of the people in the frame. And this is a great 'picture'. I know that in my gut. Christine Keeler sits with her eyes cast down. Bony. Fragile-looking. A curtain of long auburn hair falling across her cheek. Mandy Rice-Davies looks straight ahead, every inch of face visible, hair piled high in a cocky blonde beehive. Nothing fragile about Mandy. The contrast between the two personalities is right there in my lens.

But cameras were noisier back then. I manage about three shots before all hell breaks loose. The two girls hardly turn their heads, but the grumpy landlord is losing it again. For some reason, he sees them as damsels in distress and himself as their knight on a white charger. The danger is that he might grab the camera and ruin the film. Hoping he won't pursue me into the loo, I remove the film inside the shadows of my coat and replace it with another just in case he does. Out in the bar, he's yelling at my reporter who's yelling back, telling him we all need to earn a living just like he does. Then we scuttle out of there fast.

After the gloom of the pub, the smoke and the shouting, it's wonderful to reach the sunny street. I feel like a diver coming up for air. My heart is still racing, but I'm excited too. There's no denying that. And it's a scoop. No denying that either.

Back at the office, I rush to develop the negatives. Then the prints come. Those darkroom guys are geniuses. Despite the smoke and the bad lighting, the quality is fine. Bloody hell, I got it. I got a 'picture'. Tomorrow it will be on the front page, not just of my own paper but of papers in America, too. I've not been back at work long, but surely this will raise my stock no end? And it does. Though I don't know it yet, it marks the real beginning of an extraordinary career.

It's only later, when my pulse has slowed back to normal and I'm walking up the road towards my house, that my mind's eye snaps and prints a picture of myself as I'd been earlier today. Jammed in the doorway of a grubby pub loo, being shouted at and having to run for it. An unsuitable job for a woman? Some people think so; my own mother for one. An even more unsuitable job for someone who's a mother herself? Three kids, the youngest only four. Many more think that. Am I among them? It is a question I will ask myself a thousand times. Especially on those evenings when three little noses are pressed against the front window or even waiting for me outside the station.

It's that old cliché. The woman in a man's world. Trying to make her way in it. Finding her place. A bit like Christine and Mandy perhaps. The three of us. Sisters under the skin?

Chapter One

Disaster on the Doorstep

I don't remember what I was doing when he knocked at the door. What happened next has driven it from my mind.

I expect it was the usual household grind. Making the beds. Filling the washing-machine. Clearing up the breakfast things after Pierre had gone to work and the two older kids to school. Tony was nine now and Jeanne nearly seven. Catherine, only three, would have been in her playpen with her dolls and her teddy bear.

I don't suppose I had any big plans for the day. Maybe going down to the shops or for coffee with some neighbour. Perhaps taking the bus to see my mother, who lived not far away. I knew how lonely she often got when my dad was at work. I'd have to ring first though, to check she wasn't having one of her 'bad days' when she took to her bed, hid herself under the covers and nothing and nobody could persuade her to get up again. But we were all used to that by this time. A little black cloud that hovered over an otherwise happy family.

We'd been here for about two years now since we'd moved back from Paris. Shortlands, near Bromley, Kent, was a typical suburb of south London; necklaces of identikit leafy avenues draped around the commuter stations that whisked the men into the city every morning and brought them back safely again to find their supper waiting on the table. Number 6, Valley Road, was much like most of the other houses; built in the Thirties, not much style but cosy and spacious enough for three noisy children. Those children I'd longed for since I'd been a child myself.

I'd be lying if I pretended I didn't often think of that magical flat in which Pierre and I had started our married life. In the Latin Quarter, near the Pantheon and the Jardin du Luxembourg, on the top floor looking out over the rooftops of Paris, with the smell of roasting coffee wafting up from the shop on the ground floor, the street crammed with quirky little bars and restaurants, the marketplace just round the corner. Somehow, Valley Road couldn't quite compete with that. But I'd been the one who'd insisted we make our bed in England, so now I must lie in it.

The folk who lived around us were no more remarkable than the houses. Just decent people, trying to raise their kids and make ends meet. Friendly enough but, in that British way, reserved until you got to know them. Even when you did, many things would still be held back. If you had problems behind your chintz curtains, you mostly kept them to yourself. You put on your stiff upper lip and got on with it as best you could. After all, wasn't that how we'd won the war? Back then, privacy was a valued thing. You didn't wash your dirty linen in public. You certainly didn't spew out your troubles over the garden wall.

Anyway, I was lucky. Apart from that ongoing anxiety about my mother, I didn't have any troubles. I had a perfectly pleasant house, three beautiful children and a handsome Frenchman for a husband, who thrilled the female neighbours with his Maurice Chevalier accent.

So, on that ordinary suburban morning, there was no warning that everything was about to come crashing down around my head. No flashes of lightning or rolls of thunder. Just an unusually sharp knock on the front door. A strange man was standing there.

'Mrs Vandeputte?' he asked.

'Yes.'

'Mrs Pierre Vandeputte?'

'That's right. Who are you?'

'I'm a bailiff, madam,' he replied.

In those four words, everything changed. The sleepy world of a south London housewife was turned topsy-turvy, like the clothes tumbling around in my washing-machine. Suddenly, all the certainties were gone. Like feeling secure with the roof over our heads. Like being able to feed my children. Like believing my husband would never lie to me.

But he had. It seemed we owed the mortgage company a lot of money. The payments hadn't been made for months and now they wanted their house back. My first reaction was that some idiot had made a mistake. Some clerical error. My husband was a talented press photographer working in Fleet Street. He earned good money. Then the man on the doorstep handed me some papers. The words and the figures swam in front of my eyes, my brain refusing to focus on the horror of it. The man made me sign for receipt of the papers. His face was a mask. I suppose he did this ten times a day and had trained himself to show no human feeling. Then he just turned away and vanished down the street. He had left no footprints on the path. The garden looked exactly as it had fifteen minutes before. The flowers still nodded in the breeze, the bees still buzzed – as if he had never come at all.

The rest of that day passed in a mechanical haze. I remember nothing of it. The two older kids came home from school. Somehow, I gave them their tea, sent them upstairs to do their homework. Then Pierre came. I'd left the bailiff's documents on the kitchen table.

'In God's name, what does this mean, Pierre?' Where's the money gone?'

Even now, over half a century later, I cannot bring myself to describe the conversation that followed. My handsome, sophisticated Frenchman crumbled into a schoolboy caught in a particularly dreadful scrape. But there was nothing childish about this situation. This was as adult as anything could get. Always an emotional man, my husband, the rock to which I'd clung, dissolved before my eyes.

'What have you done with the money, Pierre?' I asked again.

And the truth, when at last it came spluttering out, was far worse than anything the bailiff could do to us. The truth would dominate our lives not just on that awful evening, hidden safely away behind our chintz curtains, but every day for nearly twenty years. The truth was that the money for the mortgage company and, it would turn out later, for the butcher, the baker and half a dozen others, had simply gone down my husband's throat.

He'd been drinking heavily for quite a while. I'd noticed that, but he was French after all. Didn't they all love their food and drink, that Gallic bon viveur thing? Besides, the French, unlike the British, were so much more civilised about drinking. Frenchmen could always handle their booze; as children they'd grown up used to a little wine. Nothing to worry about.

Now though, in the face of catastrophe, I realised he'd not been himself for some time. The charm and the smile had seemed a little more forced, the usual exuberance somehow muted. I'd made a few feeble attempts to uncover the cause.

'You all right, Pierre?'

'Fine.'

'Things okay at work?'

'Fine.'

If we British were famously reluctant to talk about our feelings, the French could be even worse. Instead of our stiff upper lip, my husband hid behind his bonhomie and the smoke from his eternal Gauloises. It was just two sides of the same coin.

But I didn't need to be told at least part of the problem. The trouble was it was something I didn't want to admit to myself. Pierre was homesick. I'd uprooted him from his home soil. He missed Paris, his family, the way of life he'd been used to, the way of working, too. In London, he was a fish out of water and he was gasping to find a way to cope. In his struggle, he'd turned to alcohol.

As soon as I'd first got pregnant, I'd known I'd want my kids to grow up in England. I'm not sure why it mattered so much. After all, what would have been so awful about having French children? I'd have loved them just the same. But that's how I felt. And Pierre, out of love, had agreed. He was a hugely gifted photographer, set fair for a fine career and he'd left all that behind. For me.

So now, out of a bright blue sky, there were two crises to be faced. Looming financial disaster and the serious illness of the person I loved most in the world. These days, they'd call it a double whammy.

'What on earth are we going to do?' I asked him.

He sat slumped in a chair, his eyes fixed on the floor. No answer came. But whatever the causes that had led him to this point, we'd have to deal with those later. The consequences of it were only too clear, spelt out in black and white on those terrifying pieces of paper the bailiff had left. We needed money fast.

In the grim days and weeks that followed, a clever solicitor kept disaster at bay, but that could only be a temporary reprieve. My father gave me some help too, though to him and my mother I played down the extent of our debts. I didn't mention the drinking. Apart from distressing them, I didn't want them to know that things in my marriage were less than perfect. Luckily, there was one obvious way to increase our income. Kids or no kids, I'd have to go back to work.

I'd not always been Mrs Pierre Vandeputte. Once upon a time, and it seemed like centuries ago, I'd been someone else entirely. I'd been Doreen Spooner. Like my future husband, I'd been a photographer. In fact, I'd been the first female photographer on the staff of a British national newspaper. Way back then, still a slip of a girl, I'd shot kings and queens, movie stars and some of the most famous faces of the times. With my camera, I'd travelled tens of thousands of miles from the freezing wastes of the Arctic Circle to the golden beaches of California. I'd known, and learnt from, several of the world's most iconic photographers. One or two of them had even told me I had real talent. And though the word hadn't been invented back then, I suppose I'd struck one small blow for feminism.

Yet compared to having a family, all of this had seemed almost trivial. As soon as the right bloke appeared, I'd sacrificed my career with hardly a second thought and gone back to the role with which most women were still stuck, many of them reluctantly. But who wanted glamour, travel and meeting famous people, when you could have nappies, teething and shopping in Bromley High Street? Maybe I wasn't very feminist after all.

For so long, my previous life had seemed like some old ball-gown locked away in a chest in the attic. But now, as Pierre and I sat desolate at the kitchen table, I knew that old costume would have to be taken out and dusted off to see if it might still fit. It was so ironic. In order to look after my children, I was going to have to walk away from them.

I made the call with a racing heart and not much hope.

I'd left the *Daily Mirror* under a very large black cloud. Back in 1948, they'd given me a big chance and they'd taken one too. Hiring a twenty-year-old girl to work in the rough and tumble of a tabloid newsroom had been a gamble. They'd invested time and effort in training me up and helping me find my feet. And then I'd just walked out on them. Somebody had made me a better offer, not of money but the opportunity to do something exciting. A three-month tour all over America photographing the life there. I was so dazzled by the idea I'd been unable to resist it. I don't remember some bigwig at the *Mirror* actually saying 'never darken our door again', but that was certainly the gist of it.

So now, twelve years on, it seemed like a pretty pointless phone call. It would probably be humiliating too, but I was desperate. I

braced myself as I dialled the number and asked to be put through
to the Picture Editor, a rather prickly man called Simon Clyne,
who I'd known in the old days. He was an old friend of my father's
and had once given me a teddy bear when I was a child, but I
knew he wasn't the sort to be influenced by that sort of sentiment.

'Hello, Simon? You probably won't remember me. It's Doreen
Spooner.'

'Crikey, little Doreen. Course I remember you, love. What can I
do for you?'

'I know this is a bloody cheek after all these years but, well…
I'm looking for a job.'

'But I heard you'd retired to domestic bliss, love.'

'Yes I had, but now I'd like to go back to work. Anything
going?'

'Well as it happens, love… could you start on Monday?'

You could have blown me down with the proverbial feather. I'd
made my trembling call at exactly the right moment. They were
short of a pair of hands and eyes. And I suspect that, in 1962, the
idea of being the only newspaper with a woman photographer on
the staff still had some appeal.

It was all a bit of a rush. By a second stroke of luck, I found a
nice girl who could come and look after the kids, collect them
from school and make their tea. But that weekend at our house
in Valley Road was a tough one. While the children played
happily in the garden as usual, Pierre and I were inside the
house, not talking much, going through the motions. There was
relief of course that some money would be coming in to help pay
all those bills that he'd stuffed into drawers unopened. But far
stronger emotions hung in the air too. Disgust over behaviour
which, back then, was regarded as less of an illness than a matter
of self-control. The awareness that our home was not really our
castle but actually belonged to some faceless company. Above all,
the sense of betrayal at all the deceit and the lies and the
stupidity of it. From those first joyous months in our little flat in

the Latin Quarter, how had we reached this point? The beautiful topaz engagement ring Pierre had given me suddenly looked distinctly tarnished.

But if that weekend was tough, that first Monday morning was even more difficult. It was hard to hand over my house and my children into the care of a stranger. I can still remember how I felt closing the front door behind me and walking away into a very different sort of life. Instead of the simple frock and the apron I wore to do the housework, I was dolled up in a smart blouse and tailored suit. My hair was neatly done and my nails freshly painted. I needed to look like a professional woman again. I knew from the past that you must always look smart in Fleet Street. You never knew where they might send you that day.

I walked along Valley Road looking straight ahead, so that I wouldn't see any twitching of net curtains.

'Did you see Doreen Vandeputte this morning?'

'No, dear, why?'

'All dressed up at the crack of dawn. Heading for the station.'

'Who's looking after the children?'

'I saw a strange young girl going in earlier.'

'I wonder what's happening there, then?'

'No idea. I'll keep you posted.'

The conversation played in my head as I stood on the platform at Shortlands Station, waiting for the train among a sea of sleepy faces. Some of these faces I'd get used to seeing every morning, though I might never speak to most of them. After so long, it seemed odd to be back among commuters, that strange race of people who can recite a train timetable as easily as the Lord's Prayer. I never guessed that I'd be making this same journey for the next twenty-six years.

In recent years, with three kids to worry about, I'd not spent much time in central London. Only for birthday treats, a rare visit to the theatre, that sort of thing. At first glance, the City looked much as it had always done. The great hulk of St Paul's, moored

beside the river, dominating everything. Some new tall buildings
here and there, gradually filling in the gaping cavities left by
German bombs. But still, on the whole, it was the dear old London
I'd always known. The City gents in their bowlers and pinstripes
still strode along the pavements; the office-women, with discreetly
painted faces, the lines of their nylon stockings perfectly vertical.

Yet there was something else in the air now. Intangible. Hard to
pin down. But different from the shabby, austere atmosphere of
the late Forties when I'd first walked along these streets. It was a
certain lightness, an informality that hadn't been there before. As
if the old City had loosened her stays. What all this actually
signified was simple. As I got off the train at Holborn Viaduct, I'd
walked slap bang into the Swinging Sixties.

The new *Daily Mirror* building was the very essence of it. A great
modernist monolith towering twelve storeys high above Holborn
Circus, right on the border of the City of London and the West
End. Looking up at this vast concrete castle, I was bloody
terrified. This wasn't just a new building, it was surely a new world
and I'd find that out the minute I went through those big glass
doors. What was I walking into? After twelve years, would I even
recognise the way of working? Would I be out of my depth
entirely, fired on my first day?

Up on the third floor, I entered the newsroom with Simon
Clyne. In every newspaper office, the newsroom was the
throbbing heart. This was where the news came in, by phone and
fax, in the notebooks of the reporters who'd rushed back with the
latest big story. Here the news would be examined, evaluated,
prioritised. Page four, six, eight or even, every journalist's holy
grail, the front page itself?

In the *Daily Mirror*'s shiny new building, the newsroom was
about twenty-metres long and ten wide. Beneath its low ceiling,
men in white shirts, ties loosened and sleeves rolled up, scurried
around between the endless rows of desks like mice in a maze.
Phones were ringing everywhere, typewriters tapped and pinged,

voices yelled across the vast space. But new building or not, the old familiar newsroom smell had already soaked into the walls. A unique mixture of sweat, testosterone and cigarette smoke. Back then, at least half of men didn't use a deodorant. Bri-nylon shirts were all the rage. Few houses had showers and people only bathed a couple of times a week. It wasn't a great combination. But there was a much more alluring scent in the newsroom air. The sheer excitement generated by the business of creating a paper and getting it out onto the streets of every town and village in Britain. And that could be intoxicating.

So, depending on your point of view, the newsroom was either heaven or a hellhole. Either it was in your blood or it wasn't. And that first nervous morning in 1962, I knew at once that it still flowed in mine.

Simon Clyne guided me through the labyrinth into a smaller, glass-walled space that led off the main area. The photographers' room. A bunch of men were scattered around the table. Reading the papers, drinking coffee, fiddling with cameras.

'Gentlemen, can I introduce you to Doreen Spooner?' he said.

One or two faces I recognised from the old days. Older now, usually a bit fatter. They stood up and shook hands, seemed pleased to see me. Then one of the faces I didn't know piped up.

'So what will you be doing then, dear? Typing?'

'She's a photographer,' said Simon. 'Just like you.'

'She's not!'

'She bloody is.'

'Stone me. Well, best of luck, Doreen.'

It was instantly clear that, at the *Daily Mirror* at least, nothing much had changed. Certainly not the culture of the newsroom. It wasn't an unpleasant culture exactly, it was just how things had always been and, in the minds of these men, probably the way they'd always remain. On most streets in London, everything was changing but Fleet Street wasn't one of them.

I doubt if they saw me as much competition. I wasn't expecting, or wanting, to be a superstar news photographer, sent out to the biggest stories, elbowing my way to the front of the scrum, getting my teeth knocked out for my art. I'd agreed with Simon Clyne that my work would be mostly on feature articles, just as satisfying creatively, but a bit less frenetic. A bit more, dare I say it, ladylike. I'd also made it clear I had children now and that I didn't want to be on duty at weekends or be away from home too much. To my surprise, they'd agreed but of course they paid me accordingly. There would be no starry-eyed salary but, at that moment, any salary at all was welcome.

For the next eight hours, I almost forgot Mrs Pierre Vandeputte of Valley Road, the mother of three children and the wife of a sad, troubled man with a terrible addiction. During those eight hours, Doreen Spooner rose like Lazarus from the tomb and began to breathe again. Slowly at first, sniffing the air and stretching her limbs. That first day, I was sent out on a couple of jobs, nothing too taxing. And sure enough, the old excitement was reborn too. The buzz of never knowing what was coming my way next. It could be the East End in the morning and Buckingham Palace in the afternoon. The world of the tabloid newspaper was totally unpredictable, totally absorbing.

Only a couple of times that day, when there was a moment to breathe, did my mind switch back to suburbia, to Tony and Jeanne at school, to little Catherine playing on the carpet, looking up at a strange new face and wondering where her mummy might be. When the bailiff had come to the door on that dreadful morning, he had nearly dealt us a death-blow. But, over the next few weeks, I slowly came to realise that a new life had come out of it. At times, it would be glamorous and fulfilling; at others, exhausting and frustrating. But it would never, ever, be dull.

When I got home that night, my house was tidy and my kids had been fed. Little arms were flung around me and questions asked about what I'd been doing. But it wasn't long before they went back to playing with their toys or reading *Bunty* or *The Beano*.

Kids are resilient after all. They'd cope. I could see that. But I could also see that the existence I'd cherished so much, my idea of what a woman's priorities should be, had gone and that things would never be quite the same again.

And yet… Doreen Spooner, that other half of me, was back and I knew that she mattered too. For the foreseeable future, Miss Spooner and Mrs Vandeputte would be locked in a silent combat and there would never really be a victor.

Then came the day when I'd been sitting alone in the photographers' room and that message came through.

'Those two tarts are in the Long Bar in Holborn. Better move fast.'

So I did. And Doreen Spooner was about to have one hell of a life.

Chapter Two

Snapshots of a Childhood

I will always remember the empty space where the cradle should have been. Eighty years on, I can still see it.

'Don't get upset when you go to visit Mum,' my father had warned. 'Something went wrong in her tummy and the poor little baby didn't live. Mum's a bit tired, but everything's going to be fine.'

In the hospital, my mother's face was as white as the pillows she rested on. Like Dad, she was a very small person and now, exhausted and miserable, she looked almost as childlike as me.

I was seven or eight. I'd been so looking forward to a brother or sister. I hated being an only child. This new baby was going to be like a Christmas and birthday rolled into one. I'd been so excited, but now I was desolate. The first tragedy of my short life. The first hint that the world could be a cruel and unfair place.

That cruelty was apparent even in the hospital ward in north London where my mother lay. All around her were beds filled with happy women who had delivered without a problem; cradles beside them, healthy babies crying their lungs out. There were proud new fathers, ecstatic relatives, vases of flowers, cards of congratulation. In the midst of all this joy, Mum was shipwrecked in her grief. Nowadays, such insensitivity would never be allowed, but 1930s Britain was less of a touchy-feely place.

'Cheer up now, Mrs Spooner,' said a brisk nurse. 'You'll be

back in here in a year's time with a lovely healthy baby. You mark my words.'

But she wasn't. She'd had a terrible labour giving birth to me. And now this. She'd had enough. There would never be another cradle. And I would go on being an only child.

All my life I'd loved babies. Almost from the time I stopped being one myself, I'd been besotted by them. To me, they were the most wonderful creatures imaginable. When I grew up, I was going to have as many as possible. At least six. Of course I had no idea how you actually got one, but I'd cross that bridge when I came to it. That empty space by the hospital bed haunted my dreams. Such a thing would never happen to me.

Ironically, the Spooners were a big extended family. Both my parents came from an enormous tribe of siblings. Not far away lived my three cousins, all boys. When I saw the fun they had together, the jokes, the teasing, even the fights, I was jealous. I adored them and they were always kind to me, but leaving their noisy, hectic house and going home alone was always a slightly depressing journey. Somehow, ours seemed oddly incomplete. My Mum kept it spotlessly perfect. A place for everything and everything in its place. But how I wished for muddy football boots lying around, socks on the bathroom floor, even somebody else's dolls as well as my own.

Doreen Beryl Spooner had been born on January 30, 1928. As was the norm in those days, I'd been born at home in Princes Avenue, not far from Alexandra Palace in north London. It was the year that women over twenty-one got the vote; only ten years since any woman had it at all. The year Amelia Earhart became the first woman to fly across the Atlantic, though only as a passenger; the pilot was still a man. That tells you all you need to know about 1928.

Soon though we moved a couple of miles to Churston Gardens in Bounds Green, which became my childhood home. It was a nice enough house in a not very interesting suburb, not dissimilar to my married home in later life. Like hundreds of other men, my father walked along these anonymous avenues every morning to take the Tube into the centre of the city. Unlike most of them, Len Spooner was on his way to a far more exciting world than his neat-as-a-pin home, his clipped privet hedge and his conventional appearance would suggest.

Born into an unremarkable family, Len Spooner was a remarkable man. He was clever, determined, ambitious. Common enough attributes that might have led him into an insurance company, a council office, perhaps his own small business. But Len had one extra, unexpected gene that would change his life, that of his wider family and, in the course of time, mine too. For Len Spooner was creative. He had an eye for beauty and for images of beauty. To the amazement of his family, Len got himself into an art college and eventually made his way into Fleet Street, rising to become Art Editor of the *Daily Herald*.

The *Herald* was a staunchly left-wing Labour paper, started by George Lansbury, the socialist politician (and grandfather of the famous actress Angela). Among its contributors were HG Wells and George Bernard Shaw. It became a best-selling title and Len Spooner played a big part in that. In the 1920s, most papers had still not learned how to use photographs effectively, but my Dad changed all that. He believed in the power of one image to replace a hundred words. He increased not just the number and size of the pictures but also crafted how they were used in conjunction with the words to tell a story with maximum impact. The public lapped it up. And so, not surprisingly, did professional photographers, all eager to have their work showcased in Len Spooner's *Herald*. That included some of the most famous names in the world, such as Henri Cartier-Bresson and Robert Capa. Though not a photographer himself, he understood how their minds worked. He recognised and encouraged the best talent and he got respect in return.

By the time I became a teenager, just before the war, Dad was one of the best-loved figures in Fleet Street. Everybody knew Len. He was such an easy-going man. I never once saw him lose his temper. People were drawn to him like moths around an eternally cheerful flame. Dad and I were always close. He never got the son he wanted, but he made do with me and he spoiled me rotten. I simply couldn't have had a better father. He was one of the great gifts of my life.

The simple, sunny character of my father was offset by the complexity of my mother. When Len got on the Tube every morning, he left behind a troubled soul in the house in Churston Gardens.

'Your Mum's not feeling so good today, Doreen,' he'd say quietly as he came down to breakfast. 'She's having a bit of a lie-in.'

We both knew the lie-in might last all day and that when I got home from school, she might still be in bed. It had happened now and again for as long as I could remember but, after the death of the baby, it had got a whole lot worse.

Ada Spooner's early life hadn't been easy. In fact, it had been bloody awful. She'd come from a family of six kids: four boys and two girls. Her mother had been born deaf and her grandparents lived with them too. From the age of fourteen, the young Ada found herself used as a combination of carer and skivvy.

'I used to iron thirty shirts at a time,' she'd tell me, with a warped sense of pride rather than outrage.

Of course the outrage was there too, but pushed deep below the surface, which was the trouble. She'd once been badly scalded when the spout of a boiling kettle had caught on the back of her dress and fallen off the stove. The hot water had splashed her back and legs. Her dress and stockings had to be ripped off her burnt skin in order to put iodine on the open wounds. She spent three days in hospital and she carried the scars for the rest of her days – she was very conscious of them. But the mental scarring ran deeper. Her younger sister was allowed to go out to work while Ada was kept imprisoned in the house.

And so the walls closed in on her, shutting out whatever dreams she might once have had. Despite the miraculous escape that marriage to my father brought her, she never really broke through those walls ever again. She merely swapped her parents' house for her own. Domesticity became her reason for living. Somehow, like millions of other women in those days, she persuaded herself it was the highest calling a woman could have. But in Ada's case, it went to extremes. The house became her kingdom. Obsessively, compulsively so. No charwoman would ever cross Ada Spooner's threshold. In everything else, she chose to be subservient to my father, though that wasn't his choice. Mum never made any decisions. She didn't even have a bank account. Her only real outing was a weekly shopping trip to Wood Green with one of her sisters-in-law.

When the baby died, she no doubt saw it as a failure of her responsibility to be the perfect wife. So the days in bed grew more frequent. I often wondered what she thought about as she lay there, the sunshine shut out by the curtains. Was she being eaten up with resentment at what had happened to her? Did she imagine what other sort of life she might have had?

It's clear now that Ada Spooner was clinically depressed, as we say now. Dad tried many times to get help for her. Posh doctors were consulted. Electric-shock treatment was used; a 'miracle' drug was tried but it only made her worse. There were some very dark times indeed, which I, as a child, mercifully didn't understand. She would struggle with her illness all her life and never overcame it. But yet, when she was able to leave her bed, she was a warm, caring and affectionate mother. I loved her deeply and my Dad never wavered in his adoration of her. So it was so sad to see her sunk in despair, wrestling with the demons of her rotten childhood.

Not surprisingly, my mother's problems pushed me towards the company of my father, both for companionship and for mutual comfort in the face of this grim situation. Mum must have seen this and felt excluded, which can hardly have helped her depression. For all three of us, it was a vicious circle with no escape route.

I suppose Mum's legacy to me was two-fold. It showed me that whatever dreams I might have, I must pursue them with determination or I'd end up resentful and bitter. On the other hand, her attitudes about the almost religious importance of home and children had seeped into me too. Despite my closeness to my sunny father, there was more of my damaged mother in me than I cared to admit.

Because he worried about the effects on a child of my mother's problems, Dad went out of his way to make up for it. One day when I was about eight, he brought me a new toy. It had come from Woolworths and had only cost five shillings. I soon dropped it on the ground and it smashed to pieces. But this inauspicious start wasn't any sort of omen. Quite the reverse. The present Dad gave me that day was to set the course of my life. It was a Bakelite camera.

As I got older, I began to get fascinated by the stories Dad brought home from the office; tales from his other world, a world that seemed so much more exciting than Churston Gardens and Hornsey County School. The big news events of the 1930s were the meat and potatoes of Dad's working day and, when he got home, had his supper and put his feet up, he'd sometimes try and explain them to me. The awful Mr Hitler. The Spanish Civil War. The 1936 Olympics. The latest on the two little princesses, Elizabeth and Margaret Rose. Even Edward VIII and Mrs Simpson. I never guessed that, one day, I'd photograph some of them.

Eventually, I pestered Dad to take me into the *Daily Herald*. I was shown the massive printing presses deep down in the basement; sleeping monsters by day but which would roar into life long after I'd gone to bed. I went to the newsroom and had my hand shaken and head patted by all sorts of people, who then rushed off in a dozen different directions; shouting at each other across the huge, airless room. The noise was incredible but my God it was exciting.

Dad's desk was littered with photographic prints, fresh and shiny, still smelling of the chemicals from the darkroom. Pictures of the royals, of famous sportsmen, of Hollywood film stars. Men with cameras slung over their shoulders came and went around the desk. There were fierce but good-natured rows about which photograph was the one that would go into the paper. I soon noticed that Dad always won. His word was law. He was the boss and I was so proud of being his daughter.

As the years went by, I got to know some of Dad's photographers quite well and plagued them to let me string along on their jobs. Now and again, usually when they needed a model and had no budget to pay a fee, they'd agree. Once, I stood in the midst of a field of daffodils, looking angelic. Another time, I had to pose among the chimps at the zoo. Without trying to, I slowly absorbed how a photographer worked, what his problems and challenges were and, above all, what he was trying to achieve. It was always the same thing of course. A great image. Pure and simple. He'd take an image back to the *Herald* office, slave over it in the darkroom, then triumphantly slam a print down onto my dad's desk in the hope that he'd smile and say, 'You got it.'

In this way, I met those two giants of photography: Henri Cartier-Bresson, the father of photojournalism, and Robert Capa, the great Hungarian war photographer. Both great friends of my Dad. Capa gave me one of his old Leica cameras, which even back then must have been worth a few bob. I really didn't appreciate my luck. But when I met both these men again many years later, I was glad to be able to prove that the gift hadn't been entirely wasted.

One of my father's best photographers was Jimmy Jarché (grandfather of the actor David Suchet and his brother John, the radio presenter). Jimmy had made his name capturing the first shots of Edward VIII in the company of the mysterious woman who later turned out to be Wallis Simpson. Jimmy and his family had a seaside bungalow near Clacton and Dad bought one nearby, not just for pleasure, but because it might be good for my mother to get out of the house. There were many happy times playing on the beach, eating fish and chips and hearing Dad and Jimmy swapping tales of the big scoops on which they'd been involved. Bit by bit, I was drinking it all in – the thrill and excitement of a life in Fleet Street.

But soon, our family life was blown apart by something far more serious than my mother's illness. The war came, seemingly out of nowhere on that sunny Sunday morning. September 3, 1939.

'I have to tell you now that… this country is at war with Germany,' said Neville Chamberlain in his posh voice on our big old wireless set.

At first nothing much seemed to happen. Life went on. Dad was too old to be called up to fight and was anyway in a 'reserved' profession, the press being a vital part of the war effort. But it wasn't long before we had to face the obvious fact that London was a primary target. The bombing which at first had seemed quite distant, gradually got closer to the leafy suburbs of north London.

I used to stand at the kitchen door and hear the bombs falling near Bounds Green Station, praying that Dad would be all right as he went to and from Fleet Street. Now there was an Anderson shelter in the back garden; a sort of shed thing, but made of thick corrugated iron, submerged a few feet into the ground and covered with layers of soil and thick turf. Simple bunk beds were installed inside and we Spooners, all being small, could stand up, but anyone taller than six feet had to stoop. You really couldn't swing a cat. In the winter months, there was nothing worse than hearing the air-raid sirens, then Dad dragging me out of my warm bed for a long chilly night in the shelter. Inside the house, if there wasn't time to rush for the garden, we'd cower under the Morrison shelter (a reinforced table made of metal).

These strategies saved millions of lives but London was a primary target. Soon there was a mass evacuation of children out of the capital to the safer countryside. It wasn't compulsory to send your child and my parents resisted as long as they could. But then something ghastly happened.

I've never forgotten the image of it. Just a plain white shirt. Flapping in the wind, the arms stretched wide as if to hug someone. If it had been on a washing-line, I'd never have noticed it. But it was thirty feet above the ground, snagged on the bare branches of a tree. It wasn't alone up there. There were trousers too and skirts and blouses, corsets and long-johns, socks and scarves fluttering against the calm blue sky as if they hadn't a care in the world, unconcerned by the devastation all around them. The bomb had blown the house to smithereens. Scattering its bricks, its tiles, its glass, its furniture in every direction, even the contents of its drawers and wardrobes. I shuddered to think where its people were.

The sight of that white shirt in the tree has always stayed with me. Despite the horror that it represented, I found myself entranced by it. How terrible it was, but how strangely beautiful too. The sad, lost shirt, tugging in the wind to set itself free and get back down to earth where it belonged. I was only about twelve, but already the power of images had a tight hold on me.

But it was too much for my father.

'Doreen, I think it's high time we got you to safety,' he said.

'Oh no, Dad, I'll be all right. I'm sure I will.'

'No, love. We'd rather lose you for a little while than forever. You've got to go now, Doreen.'

It was pretty awful saying goodbye to Mum and Dad on the platform at King's Cross Station. But tens of thousands of other kids were going through the same thing, so I tried to be brave. Luckily, a whole gang of us from Hornsey County School was evacuated as a group to Wisbech in Cambridgeshire, so I wasn't exactly alone. Even better, my three boy cousins weren't far away. So it could have been worse.

In fact, I struck lucky and was billeted with a lovely family called the Clarks. They owned no less than three music shops in the town and their house was far grander than Churston Gardens. It almost seemed like I'd checked into the Ritz. Their daughter Fay and I got along at once. She had no resentment at this interloper who'd invaded her home. At last I had a sort of sister and we became friends for life.

I soon infected Fay with my passion for photography. By now we both had Kodak pull-out cameras and we buzzed around the town snapping everything in sight, not just people but also the lovely landscape along the banks of the River Nene. Still, it was babies who fascinated me most, particularly the ever-changing expressions on those pudgy little faces. I fantasised about owning my own studio one day and photographing them non-stop, an endless conveyor belt of gurgling fun.

Mr Clark was a kind and funny man. When Mum and Dad first came to visit, he dressed up in a wicked-witch costume with a wig and make-up so he could go 'boo!' to them at the front door. Fay and I raised money for the Red Cross by creating a swear-box into which he had to put sixpence when he used a bad word, belched or broke wind. There was even a dishy elder brother on whom I developed a massive crush whenever he came home from boarding school. He was Clark Gable, Leslie Howard and Ronald Colman rolled into one. Swoon.

I was now at that time of life when a girl starts looking at boys in a different way and needs her mother to guide and explain. However affectionate and maternal Mrs Clark tried to be, it wasn't the same. I worried constantly about my parents too, living right at the bullseye of Hitler's bombs. Any day, through the letterbox of that grand house in Wisbech, a telegram could have come telling me that Churston Gardens had been blown to bits, my parents killed and that I was now an orphan. I tried not to picture Dad's shirts or Mum's blouses fluttering in the branches of a tree.

But by 1944, the bombings on London had grown less intense and my parents agreed that I could go back to London. In the future, many evacuee children would tell grim tales of misery, neglect and even abuse in their wartime foster homes, but I had had nothing but kindness and care. I would never forget it.

Churston Gardens still stood unscathed and I slipped back into my former life like a comfy old slipper. The joy of having me back cheered my mother to such an extent that, for a while at least, there were fewer 'bad days'. Dad was still at the peak of his profession, earning pretty good money and they'd enrolled me at posh all-girl Tollington High School in Muswell Hill. But for once I rebelled. I'd only just discovered boys. What was the logic of turning my back on them now? So I went to Hornsey Grammar School, where I was eventually voted Head Girl, heaven knows why. The war wasn't over yet and senior pupils had to do some 'firewatch' duty at nights, sleeping in the school in case of enemy activity. We had to have the stirrup-pumps all ready to tackle any blaze. It never happened, thank God. I'd have been bloody useless at putting out a fire.

I left school at the age of sixteen, perfectly common for a girl back then. I had no interest in going to university, nor to the poncey finishing-school my parents had been toying with. I didn't even want to sit what are now called 'A' Levels, which didn't please my Dad. But what was the point of exams, universities or finishing schools? Especially when the headmaster told me that I was really only qualified to work in the Women's Land Army, an organisation that drafted women to work in the fields to help feed Britain in wartime and after. Well, he could stuff that for a start. Nor was I heading for a secretarial course so I could sit typing in some gloomy office until I found a husband. Oh no, not me.

Miss Doreen Spooner of Bounds Green already knew perfectly well what she wanted to do with her life. Somebody else could dig to feed Britain. Miss Spooner was planning to feed her imagination by capturing images of the world as she saw it. For a while at least, those six babies must stay as a twinkle in the eye of my unknown Romeo.

Chapter Three

My University of Photography

I stood completely alone in the middle of a vast and empty
landscape. It was flat, frozen and stretched away to a distant
horizon, above which hung a weak and watery sun. It was
beautiful and terrifying at the same time. This was Lapland,
inside the Arctic Circle. A hell of a long way from Bounds Green.

I was on skis, a method of transport on which I could do little
more than trudge. I'd covered about three long miles by now, with
a camera bag over my shoulder and I was getting pretty tired. I
was a twenty-year-old London girl for heaven's sake, not bloody
Captain Scott. Till now, my idea of the middle-of-nowhere had
been Clacton. This was something else.

But this was where the annual roundup of the reindeer was
happening, or so they'd told me back at the travellers' lodge.
That'd make some nice pictures for you, Doreen, they'd said. So
off I went. You're daft when you're young.

Eventually I found them in the distance, or rather I heard them
first. A big circle of Sami men and a huge herd of reindeer. The
men were trying to lasso the animals and bring them in for
branding. It was a noisy business; the shouts of the men, the
bellowing of the deer. It was gory too. When a sick or very old
animal was discovered, its throat was swiftly cut and blood gushed
out onto the snow. But the images were stunning. The dark figures

of the men against the emptiness of the crystal-white landscape as they tried to scratch some kind of living. The horns of the reindeer, like crowns on their heads, bucking and tossing as they tried to evade capture.

I stayed at a distance, using my zoom lens. The Sami men saw me, but they paid me no heed. I suppose, if I'd thought hard about it, I'd have realised how vulnerable I was. But all I could think of was that these were going to be the best pictures I'd ever taken. And they were. Later, they'd be wired back to my father in London and eventually published.

That trudge into the wilderness was a special day in my life. A road to Damascus in fact, though in a less appealing climate. It was the day when the penny really dropped that taking photographs could be an extraordinary window on life. Standing there alone in Lapland, shooting the reindeer roundup, suddenly seemed like the most amazing thing for a girl like me to be doing. An incredible privilege. How far was this, not just from my suburban existence in London, but from the existence of my own mother and millions of women like her? How far too from the typing-pool or a nice job behind the haberdashery counter of Swan & Edgar?

As I half-fell back through the door of the travellers' lodge, I was exhilarated by the possibilities that lay in front of me if I had the guts to reach out for them. This photography lark might take you anywhere, show you things you never dreamed you'd see. For the first time, I realised it could be about a lot more than snapping babies in long lace shawls.

But it had taken me quite a while to come to this realisation. Well before I'd left school, there had been the inevitable conversation with Dad.

'Right then,' he said, 'If you don't fancy the Women's Land Army, what's it going to be? You can't sit on your bottom around here.'

'You know what it's going to be,' I said.

'Oh, do I? And what's that then?'

We both knew the answer quite well. I could see the glint in his eye, the smile half-formed on his lips, but he was going to make me say it.

'A photographer.'

'But you're a girl.'

'So what?'

'It'll be tougher for a girl,' he said. 'People expect a bloke. They trust a bloke.'

'So what?' I said again.

'Christenings, weddings and the like?'

'I suppose so. For a start, anyway.'

'You're sure?'

'I'm sure.'

'OK,' he said.

There was a photographic school run by the London County Council at Bolt Court, just off Fleet Street. Despite the location, it didn't teach anything about press photography, just the basics of how cameras work, how to shoot pictures, how to develop and print them. Here I learned how to judge the quality of light and the depth of focus; what lenses delivered different length of focus; which apertures were the right width for which sort of shot; and a hundred other basics of the photographer's trade.

The course fees weren't high and there were a few other girls there too, so I wasn't a freak. But all of them had a very clear idea of the work they wanted to do: in a warm, cosy studio, doing elegant portraiture of people all dressed-up in their Sunday best. Titled debutantes and their aristocratic mothers, the sort of thing you still see in *Country Life*. Babies too, of course, just as I wanted to do.

There was a snobbery at Bolt Court and the thing looked down upon was press photography. All these people really wanted to create were pretty paintings. Smooth, glossy images of bland perfection, shot beside an urn filled with roses or a pair of fake

French windows. Their idols were the great portrait photographers like Cecil Beaton and Lenare. Not for them the rough and tumble of the real world, life as it really was. Press work was simply not seen as 'good' photography. It was scruffy, sleazy, distinctly downmarket. It was certainly no job for a 'lady'.

But this daughter of the Spooner dynasty had Fleet Street in her blood. I'd stood beside my father's desk in the *Daily Herald*, seen the talent, craft and dedication that went into every picture that appeared in a newspaper. I'd listened to the tales of Dad and Jimmy Jarché as they sat on the sands at Clacton. Without a splinter of a doubt, I knew that press photography was something to be admired. Something far more exciting, vivid and alive than spending everyday looking through the lens at some posh debutante sitting on a gilt chair with a frozen smile that looked like she had a stick of rock up her arse.

So, just as when I'd left school, I left Bolt Court before taking the course exams. Looking back, it was arrogant and wrong, but I simply felt they had nothing more to teach me. One day, the newspaper industry would start their own school for training press photographers, but that was far in the future. I knew the only way I'd learn would be on the job. My final walk down that cramped little alleyway of Bolt Court and out into the long sweep of Fleet Street was symbolic. A blast of fresh air in every sense.

I'd always been determined to make it as a photographer, without any help from my father. Noble, but a bit naïve. He arranged what we'd now call 'work experience' with a news photographer friend – going out with him on his jobs, holding his bags, getting him cups of coffee. The usual scenario. The lowest of the low. But I loved every minute. The days flew by, always different, always interesting. Now, at last I was seeing how living, breathing photographers worked. And it was a revelation. Then came a surprising invitation.

'No, Doreen, you can't go. I'm not having it. It's out of the question,' said my mother.

'She'll be fine, Ada. She's a big girl now,' replied my father.

'That's right. Gang up on me, the two of you. You always do,' she said.

The offer came from one of Dad's celebrated friends, the great Swedish photographer Karl Gullers. To go to Stockholm for a few months, work with him and learn my trade. A sort of traineeship.

Gullers was a lovely man, six-foot four, a big, warm teddy bear. I knew him well too. He'd often stayed at our house when he'd come over to London selling his pictures to my Dad and the other picture editors on Fleet Street. He thought the British were very eccentric and couldn't believe the amount of tea we drank.

'For God's sake, Ada, no more tea!' he'd cry as Mum offered him yet another.

Karl Gullers' photographs of Scandinavia, its spectacular landscape and the lives of its people, were admired across the world (they still are). His offer to be my mentor was an incredibly generous one. Dad knew that, but of course my Mum didn't. Because she couldn't imagine doing such a thing herself, she couldn't imagine me doing it, either. Oh, what horrors might befall me! Living among foreigners, not speaking the lingo. Far better to stay at home in Churston Gardens in the safe, secure, perfectly dusted rooms in which she spent her own days, watching her life pass by in the ticking of the ormolu clock on the mantelpiece.

On the day I hugged her goodbye, I wasn't as brave as I tried to look but nothing was going to stop me. And Stockholm was so beautiful, a city built on an archipelago on the edge of the Baltic. A place of countless islands, pretty bridges and old cobblestone streets. After dirty, black, war-battered London, it looked as if it had just been freshly scrubbed, the air clear and bracing. And, thank God, nearly everyone spoke English. I was billeted in a small flat near the Gullers family home. His wife was kind and welcoming and they had a large number of adorable young children. She'd even won a prize as Sweden's ideal mother. I was in my element, drowning in nappies, potties and prams.

I learnt so much from Karl. His studio made those I'd seen in the UK look like slums. Above all, I'd never seen such quality of prints. So bold, so perfect in every detail. The images jumped out at you and grabbed you by the lapels. It was here I learnt how much a photographer depends on the skill of technicians. Some people could be snooty with the darkroom boys, thinking of them as failed photographers, but that wasn't true. I soon realised it was their talent that could make or break the pictures you'd strived so hard to achieve. It was all about teamwork and any photographer who didn't realise that was a fool. The great names always did – Cartier-Bresson, Robert Capa and certainly Karl Gullers.

'Please, come home soon,' said Mum's letters. 'I've got nobody to talk to you without you.'

It was always her bleat that Dad didn't talk to her enough. I suppose when he got home from the *Daily Herald*, he'd been yelling his head off all day long across that heaving newsroom and longed for some peace and quiet. It probably never struck him that my mother had only spoken to the milkman, and the butcher's boy all day long. Later, I discovered she'd been so lonely, she'd coaxed the kind-hearted boyfriend of my chum Madge to go in for coffee at least once a week.

I'm ashamed to say I wasn't listening to the letters from home. I'd certainly been homesick at first, but that soon wore off. I met a nice girl of my own age who wanted to be a journalist. We did a few little jobs together and shared a flat for a while. By now, Karl was sending me out on little projects and giving me a critique on the results. Ten minutes listening to him was worth ten months back at Bolt Court.

Still obsessed by babies, I asked Karl if he could arrange for me to photograph Sweden's most important baby, the infant royal prince. An awful cheek really, but somehow he fixed it up and off I went nervously to the palace. The little prince was delightful, but tragic too. His father had been killed in an air crash the year before, a fact the child was too young to understand. It was sad to see him so happy and full of life, unaware of the shadow that hung over him. He was as lively as any two year old and not keen on sitting still, so was dragging his small chair all over the room. It took quite a while to get him to sit on it, but when he finally did, he sat on it like a throne, even if accompanied by his teddy bear. I'm glad to say that, as King Carl Gustaf, he still sits on it today at the age of seventy (nothing makes a photographer feel older than seeing her babies getting old too.)

Soon after that, Karl suggested I make the trip up to Lapland. Perhaps by now he sensed that I was capable of more than I imagined. Perhaps he thought it was time to throw me in at the deep end or, in this case, onto the cold, frozen wastes and see what happened. Whichever the reason, it worked. I never saw the world in quite the same way again.

In London, my father had sent the reindeer pictures to the Keystone Picture Agency and, when I returned from Sweden, they offered me a job. I was very much a junior and paid just £5 a week. But it was another few steps along my learning curve and here I found my next mentor, the great George König.

Like Karl Gullers, George König thought it really important to 'bring on' young people in the business. He taught me so many things, especially the vital importance of lighting. The classic example is how to photograph an egg in an eggcup. Everything depends on how it is lit. Use too much and you end up with a boring picture, because you have drenched out all its shape and texture. The trick is to use light and shade to turn a two dimensional object into three, an object of shadow as well as illumination, and therefore far more interesting and even mysterious. Of course you can also try it with a bald man.

Dear George let me trot around after him as his pupil, watching what he did but letting me take my own shots too. It was bloody brilliant. I'll never forget going with him to the Savoy Hotel to shoot the teenage Elizabeth Taylor. I just couldn't believe how

beautiful she was. In later years, when they chose her as
Cleopatra, they certainly got the casting right. Those deep violet
eyes were incredible. I've never photographed anything like them,
before or since.

My Damascene conversion in Lapland hadn't been a dead end,
merely a beginning of the long road on which I was meeting
people like George König, avidly reading *Life* magazine to see the
latest wonderful pictures of Margaret Bourke-White, really the
only notable woman press photographer of those years. All this
was my education, my university of photography. All the time, my
imagination was stretching wider, grasping the wonders that could
be achieved through the lens of a camera.

In 1948, the *Daily Mirror* decided to open its own picture agency,
to save itself the cost of using companies like Keystone. To find
their staff, they poached from the existing agencies and they
offered me a job at the grand sum of six guineas a week. How
posh that sounded, so much better than pounds, shillings and
pence. I felt a bit disloyal to Keystone but I already understood
from my Dad that Fleet Street was a tough old game and that you
had to look after yourself. And at last I'd be working for a real,
copper-bottomed newspaper. Well almost. The picture agency was
in the same building as the paper but on a different floor and the
two didn't really mingle. So I wasn't quite there yet, but at least I
was heading in the right direction.

They gave me all sorts of work to do, though always features as
opposed to news. That suited me just fine. My education went on.
There was always something new to find out; like opening one
Russian doll after another. But the agency didn't last long. It
wasn't well-run and just didn't make enough money, so the *Mirror*
shut it down. They offered jobs on the paper itself to three of the
ten agency photographers and, to my astonishment, I was one.

Dad was thrilled to bits. He hugged me so hard I thought my
bones would break.

'I can't believe it,' he kept saying. 'A photographer on a proper paper. Would you credit it? My daughter.'

A son would have been preferable of course, but a daughter was still pretty damned good. There were quite a few toasts drunk in Churston Gardens that night.

I think even my mother was proud, though she was more subdued. I wondered what she was thinking, watching me being launched into a new life. Was she envious? Remembering again the day her sister had been allowed to go off to work while poor little Ada had been forced to stay at home among the pots and pans, a suburban Cinderella?

But Britain was changing. The war had seen to that. The decade after VE Day in 1945 was a difficult one. The country was exhausted, rationing was still in force, families had been devastated by loss. The voters had booted out Churchill and replaced him with a Labour government under Clement Attlee. Many people wanted something new, a different sort of society. Most women certainly did. During the war, many had been dragged out of domesticity to work in factories, on farms and in the forces too. Now, in this brave new world, huge numbers of them didn't want to go back to the cooking and the cleaning. They wanted something a bit more challenging. And whatever my yearning for a family, I was emphatically one of those. That night, as I clinked glasses with Mum, she probably thought I was finally lost to her forever. And I suppose, in a way, that was true.

A couple of girls before me had been very briefly tried out on Fleet Street as a photographer, but they just couldn't stay the course. I was the one who lasted. I was a Spooner after all and the women, on my father's side at least, were tough as old boots. At the age of ninety, my grandmother had fallen backwards out of a first-floor window and survived. At the age of twenty, I hardly thought of myself as a tough old boot, but I suppose that's what I was.

I was glad to be going to the *Daily Mirror*. I didn't want mutterings of nepotism and, by now, there was hardly a Fleet

Street paper without a Spooner working there: Dad on the *Daily Herald*, Uncle Frank on the *Daily Express* and various cousins ensconced elsewhere. But the *Mirror* was virgin territory, so to speak.

Appropriately enough, the *Daily Mirror* in 1903 had been started as the first newspaper targeted at women. There wasn't much actual news; mostly fashion, cookery, flower-arranging, running your house and servants on a budget. That sort of thing. The advertisers were mostly the jewellers, furriers and big department stores of the West End. It was even called the *Mirror* because it was assumed most women spent their days gazing at their reflection. Its laudable mission was to be 'entertaining without being frivolous and serious without being dull'. But the Edwardian ladies hadn't taken to it and daily sales, after a flying start, had soon crashed like Icarus. So it rapidly changed tack, cut its cost to a halfpenny and relaunched itself as a picture paper for both sexes. Over time, the new revamped *Daily Mirror* would emerge as a hugely popular newspaper for the masses – easily digestible, not too heavy and, luckily for the likes of me, full of photographs.

But by that day in 1949 when I first walked into the *Mirror* offices, then still in a shabby old building off Fetter Lane, there was nothing remotely fragrant or feminine about the world of newspapers. Along with the bullrings of Spain, it was probably the most macho environment imaginable. Instead of vanquishing a bull, the enemy in a newspaper office is the clock. Six days a week, a new edition has to go to press every single evening. From first thing in the morning till the moment those giant printing presses start to hum, everything is directed towards that objective.

There was never any time for people's finer feelings. You could get bruised, battered even. Your ego could end up bleeding, with its face in the sand.

'For God's sake, Doreen, my cat could take a more exciting picture than that!'

Even really tough men, blokes who'd just come through the

horrors of war, could find it daunting. That's probably why so
many of them leant heavily on the crutches of cigarettes and
booze. The hot, heaving newsroom often smelt like a pub before
closing time.

I knew that my being a woman wasn't likely to make much
difference. These guys weren't going to change at the first sight of
my pretty legs or at a whiff of my Coty perfume. If I really wanted
to enter the bullring, I'd have to take whatever darts were thrown
at me. I'll not say I wasn't nervous, but I was also too excited to let
it matter.

On that first morning, Dad and I took the Tube together from
Bounds Green down into the City. He gave me a hug as we went
our separate ways.

'Welcome to Fleet Street, love,' he said. 'You can do it. I know
you can.'

When I was taken into the photographers' room to be
introduced, the ten or so men were very polite, but a bit reserved.
It was as if Princess Elizabeth had walked in. Perhaps they
thought their little world had come to an end, that they'd have to
roll down their shirt-sleeves, straighten their backs and remember
to wash their hands when they went for a pee. Maybe, they
worried that I might get the best jobs by flirting with the Picture
Editor. Wasn't that the sort of thing women did?

But there was no time to worry about any of that now. The
clock was ticking. Tomorrow's paper had to be put together.
Reports were rushing in, by phone and through the wires. Stories
were happening out there and we had to go and get them. By
tomorrow morning all of it had to be on the breakfast tables of
Britain beside the teapot, the toast and the porridge. There was no
time to waste. Nothing else mattered. Certainly not the first-day
nerves of some girl photographer.

I got sent out on three jobs that day. All three of them were
different and interesting. And, by beginner's luck, all three of them
got into the paper next day. The blokes in the photographers'

room were a teeny bit less standoffish the next morning. One of them even pulled out a chair for me. Not long after, my shot of the playwright George Bernard Shaw peering at me through his garden gate won a prize as a 'British News Picture of The Year'.

Maybe that clinched it. One day, I walked into the photographers' room to find them all waiting and a big cake on the table.

'Doreen, we've tried every trick in the book to test you,' their spokesman said, 'and you've passed with flying colours. Welcome aboard.'

There was applause. I smiled graciously, cut the cake and gave them all a slice in my most ladylike manner. I didn't want to spoil their fun by telling them I hadn't a bloody clue what they were on about. Whatever schoolboy tricks they'd tried, I hadn't noticed a single one of them. Water off a duck's back.

The only thing that did ruffle my feathers was when my shots appeared in the paper with the caption 'Picture by Camera Girl Doreen Spooner'. I didn't like that at all.

'What's it going to say when I'm older?' I protested to the Picture Editor. 'Camera Granny?'

They didn't do it again after that. Bloody cheek. Though I guess they meant it to be endearing, rather than chauvinistic. But I wasn't having it.

It had been nearly two years since my road-to-Damascus moment up in the Arctic Circle. But I still sometimes looked at those photographs of the reindeer. I'd learnt two lessons on that Lapland day that would stay with me for life. First, that to get your great picture, you've sometimes got to trudge a fair distance, whether it's across frozen Arctic wastes, along the Great Wall of China or just into the unused reaches of your own imagination. Second, when you know in your soul that you've captured it, nothing else, apart from maybe sex and babies, will ever come close.

Chapter Four

Miss Spooner
Spreads Her Wings

Albert Einstein was glaring at me. He wasn't a happy bunny. I was pointing a camera at him and my chances of getting a smile were clearly negligible. But that didn't matter. It was such a great face, wrinkled like an old paper bag, clouds of wild grey hair blowing round it in the breeze. My finger itched to press the shutter.

We'd just gone up to the house and rung his bell. We'd been expecting some maid to open it, but there was Albert himself, the world's greatest physicist, one of the towering intellects of the 20th century. And looking very grumpy. Maybe we'd interrupted him while he worked on a new theory. My companion introduced us, explained that we were touring the USA, compiling a library of photographs of its way of life and of prominent Americans. These would be sold on to magazines in Europe, so that they could get a clearer understanding of the greatest country in the world. You'd have thought Albert would be in favour of this, but my friend had made one mistake. A big one. He'd spoken to Einstein in German. The Jewish physicist had fled his home country when Hitler came to power and never gone back. Nowadays, he was as American as apple pie and baseball. One of his great friends was Charlie Chaplin. Albert's front door was politely but firmly closed in our faces. But not before I'd got a few shots.

My Mum would have been mortified. If Mr Einstein had declined to be interviewed or photographed, then I should have thanked him and walked away, carefully closing the gate behind me. Taking some unapproved pictures was hardly the action of a lady. But by that stage, I'd managed to suppress most of those qualms. I'd not have survived long as a press photographer if I hadn't. I'd never quite develop the rhino hide of today's paparazzi, but I knew when you had to be a bit impolite, push your luck, see how much you could get away with.

Anyway, I was having such fun. Six-thousand miles from home, cruising round the States for three whole months in a big, flash Oldsmobile car. Only twenty-two, it was the experience of a lifetime. I'd known it would be. But it had been a big decision to grasp it.

'Well, young woman, if you leave now, you'll not be coming back,' someone in authority at the *Daily Mirror* had said.

I could hardly blame him. They'd given me a chance, steered and nurtured me, given me varied and interesting work. I'd been accepted as a player in that wild, exhilarating environment and I was grateful to them for so much. And now I was throwing it back in their faces. 'Look, I'm only twenty,' I'd said. 'I really want to take this chance. It might never come again. Please try to understand.' But when I walked away down Fetter Lane on my last day, I visualised a big black cartoon cloud hanging above my head.

Mum, of course, thought I was crazy. But Dad had been supportive, though I suspect he felt the same way.

'If you're sure it's what you want,' he said. 'You've only got the one life.'

But I think he had another, unspoken motive. My parents had left north London by now and moved down south to Beckenham. God knows why. This had separated my mother from the extended family and made her depression a lot worse. 'Good' days were far fewer. She went to bed every afternoon now and he never knew what he'd find when got home from Fleet Street. Maybe he felt it was best for me to be out of the way for a while.

The offer had come out of the proverbial blue. Bert Garai, my old employer at the Keystone Picture Agency, still remembered me. He was planning his great project and thought I'd fit in. It would just be the four of us. Bert, his wife and his son, who was a features writer. As well as taking pictures, I'd be female company for his wife and, I suspect, for his son, young Bertram (though nothing whatever came of that).

Bert Garai sniffed a big marketing opportunity. After the six years of wartime misery, there was a real appetite in Europe for the things of life that had been denied them for so long. That included magazines and these were springing up all over the place. America, to many Europeans still trying to rebuild their war-ravaged cities, seemed like the promised land. So shiny and prosperous, so excitingly fresh and different. And they wanted the magazines to show them more of it.

In New York, Bert bought this glorious Oldsmobile car, all plush and shiny with sharp metal tail fins, and off we went. Over the next three months, we'd cover about 25,000 miles. Bert had planned a detailed itinerary across America, based on magazine features he thought he could sell to Europe. It was an interesting time in the States, right on the cusp of the 1950s. We did a big piece on 'Teenagers in America' and one of my photographs won a prize as 'a perfect visualisation of the spirit of the USA'. It was a culture that seemed so much more vibrant and refreshing than anything going on back in stuffy old Europe. I loved it. We went to Las Vegas, an exploding kaleidoscope of colour and light, which made Blackpool look like a damp squib. We did a feature on 'instant marriage' – you could decide to get spliced at breakfast time and be tucked up in the honeymoon suite by lunch.

But it wasn't all fun or admirable. My horizons were widened pretty damn quick, especially when we went down into the Deep South and I saw, for the first time in my life, the terrible oppression of black people. The conditions they lived and worked in were sometimes dreadful. The drudgery of the cotton fields was truly grim, as if slavery had never really been abolished. One poor young girl begged me to take her away with me. She'd be my maid, do anything at all. She didn't want paying, just an escape from oppression and a hope of something better. It was awful. I could never forget her face and always wondered what had happened to her. Though maybe it was better not to know. Long afterwards, I was photographing the great singer Lena Horne when she came to the London Palladium and I told her the story.

'Honey,' she said with a slow sigh, 'that was just the way it was.'

We stayed in so many motels, they began to blur into one. But I loved life on the road. And Bert had planned our destinations well. Every place we stopped there seemed to be wonderful new stories and images waiting to fall into our laps like ripe plums. My camera lapped up American life. I photographed men in smoky bars, drinking and playing pool; horses at the rodeo; gamblers at the roulette wheels; housewives in glossy kitchens with space-age appliances that made ours back home look like antiques.

The landscapes, too, were so alien and fascinating after cramped little Britain: endless prairies of waving corn as far as the horizon; the thundery swamplands of the South; the wild, barren peaks of the West. I even climbed up Crazy Horse Mountain to see the huge face of the Indian chieftain being gradually carved out of the rock. It was a hell of a climb up sheer rocky paths in the blazing heat of the Black Hills of Dakota, but I made it. There was no way I was going to miss getting a picture. (Years later, my *Mirror* colleague Kent Gavin gave up halfway. Back at the bottom, a guide told him, 'Gee, you're not very tough. We had a young English girl once who got right to the top in no time.' Kent never forgave me for that.)

Eventually, the Oldsmobile, pretty dusty by now, reached the Pacific coast and that famous 'Hollywood' sign rising above Los Angeles. It was the height of the studio system, before the advent of television put an end to the golden age. The huge film factories still churned out hundreds of movies a year. The stars were like gods, worshipped all over the world. Humphrey Bogart, Clark Gable, Cary Grant; Bette Davis, Greer Garson, Joan Crawford. How I longed to point my lens at some of the greats, but sadly Bert had only managed to book a few 'B List' types, a slightly tedious parade of pretty starlets, male and female, whose good looks were all they had to recommend them. Most had posed for a half a dozen other photographers that week and were dead behind the eyes. This was something I'd often have to cope with throughout my career, the professional model who believed their physical beauty was enough to make them alluring and had nothing else to give. Mannequins with a pulse. I'd rather have had Albert Einstein's wrinkles and pouches anytime. But Hollywood was an extraordinary place, a bizarre sort of paradise. Not surprisingly, in view of its purpose, it seemed totally fake, simply not in the real world. 'Tinseltown' and no mistake.

By far the most satisfying of my American photographs were in total contrast to the sunshine and fleshpots of Beverly Hills. The Amish community were, and still are, a conservative Christian sect that had mostly withdrawn from modern life and lived in small shut-off corners of Pennsylvania. To a photographer's eye, they were definitely a gift from God. Their villages were like something from the previous century. Nothing mechanical was allowed. Instead of tractors, they farmed by horse and plough. Cars were banned. The basic transport was by horse and buggy. Their clothes were straight out of *Huckleberry Finn*. Shoes on children were considered unnecessary until they were fully grown. Young men had to be married by the age of twenty, after which time they never shaved their chins. The women wore no make-up, their hair never knew a curler or a perm. Personal vanity was abhorred and that included having your picture taken, so I had to be discreet.

The Sunday service was the very heart of their lives. They had no churches, but simply joined together in a different farmhouse every week. By hook or crook, probably the latter, we found out where the next service was going to take place and I got up early one Sunday to catch them heading there. They saw me, of course, but said nothing and certainly didn't try to stop me. That would not have been their way. I kept my distance and tried to be respectful, but I felt more intrusive than I ever had before. In their minds, I felt sure, I was being judged and found wanting, a misguided woman from the wicked outside world who had strayed from the path of righteousness and whose values had been warped by the lure of Mammon. My mother's face flashed before me again – she wouldn't have approved either. It was one thing to be a bit pushy with film stars, politicians or even Albert Einstein, but these were simple people who only asked to be left alone to follow their faith. And here was little Doreen Spooner literally sticking her nose in.

Of course it was the dilemma of every newspaper person. It still is. How far do you go? Where is the line you don't cross? No doubt the answer is different for everyone, but it was that Sunday morning in Pennsylvania that confirmed my suspicion that I would never want to do really heavy news work. I'd never make a good 'door-stepper', a thruster and a pusher. I don't believe that was down to my gender, just my nature.

But oh, the pictures that came out of that uncomfortable morning. I was so proud of them, even more than of the reindeer in Lapland. By some miracle, I felt I'd somehow 'got' the essence of these unusual people. The images seemed as pure and simple as they were and I hoped that, when they were published, they might intrigue the readers, make them want to better understand a very different approach to life and so maybe, just maybe, justify my intrusion.

It had been an incredible three months. When we got back to New York, Bert sold the beloved Oldsmobile and headed back with his wife and son to Britain. About to be unemployed, I'd rather hoped he might offer me a permanent job at Keystone in London, but he had a full complement there so he didn't. There were no hard feelings. I'd accepted his offer with my eyes wide open and he'd given me exactly what I'd hoped for – an unforgettable experience and a chance to grow as a photographer. I couldn't complain. I regretted nothing.

I hung on in New York for a few weeks, staying with an old chum from the *Daily Mirror* who'd moved there with his wife. After three months constantly on the road, it was bliss to sleep in the same bed for a while and to get to know that spectacular city.

No matter how many times you've seen it in movies or in magazines, nothing quite prepares you, especially if you're a photographer. Every time you turn your head, there's some fresh image you simply must capture. Not just the mind-boggling buildings scarping the clouds, but the vignettes of life down on the pavements, the yellow cabs, the manhole-covers hissing steam, the women shopping at Bloomingdale's, the commuter crowds surging off the Staten Island Ferry. My hostess owned a Siamese cat and I persuaded her to put it on a lead and walk down Fifth Avenue while I snapped away. Boy, did heads turn, even in tough old New York. She looked a million dollars and so did the Siamese, especially when it tried to climb up the drainpipe of Cartier, the jewellers. It was one cool cat.

America was unforgettable. I was bowled over by the sheer size of it and by all the opportunities it had offered me to go on learning my trade. Coming from an often drab post-war Britain, where bread was still rationed, it seemed like the land of milk and honey. I felt it had put a spring in my step and a new sparkle in my work. I'd always be grateful to it for that.

On leaving, I watched the towers of Manhattan fade away with a sad heart. It was time to go home and face the music. The big question was what the bloody hell did I do now?

England seemed so small when I got back. Even mighty London felt a bit like Toytown after New York. At home in Beckenham, things hadn't improved, though my return seemed to perk Mum up for a little while. Her spotless living room with everything in its place seemed so claustrophobic after being in the back of the Oldsmobile, on the open road, with the wind off the prairie blowing through my hair.

It would have been nice to be going back into the *Daily Mirror*, but I'd made my bed and now I must lie in it, though always hoping to hear the phone ringing downstairs with the offer of some work. The paradox was that I'd come back from America believing I was a far better photographer than when I left, and now I didn't have a job. Dear old Dad networked for me and a few bits and pieces dribbled in but nothing of much interest.

'I told you so,' said Mum. 'Running off to America like that. Throwing away a good steady job, which was more than I ever had the chance of. Well, your chickens are coming home to roost now.'

One day when, as usual, the phone wasn't ringing, I rang somebody instead. It was long-distance, what was then called a 'trunk call', so I did it when Mum had gone to the shops. Audrey Whiting, another old friend from the *Mirror*, was one of the most promising journalists of her day. That's why, at the age of only twenty-three, the *Daily Mirror* had made her their correspondent in Paris. I really just called for someone to talk to, but that call changed everything.

'What are you up to then, Doreen?'

'Not much. A bit here, a bit there.'

'Well get yourself on the next ferry. There's plenty of freelance work over here.'

'Come to Paris? Where would I stay?'

'Stay with me. For a while, anyway.'

'But my French is pathetic.'

'Doesn't matter. You'll pick it up. Come on, it'll be fun.'

I dithered for a moment. I glanced along my mother's immaculate hallway into her immaculate living-room: two chintz armchairs sat in front of the fireplace; their matching cushions, plumped up like fat pigeons, positioned precisely to support the weary back. There wasn't a sound in the house apart from the ticking of the ormolu clock on the mantel. It seemed, as they say these days, a no-brainer.

'You're on,' I said, slightly aghast as I heard myself say it.

'Brilliant. Oh, and Doreen?'

'Yes?'

'There's somebody here I'd really love you to meet.'

Chapter Five

The Princess, the Duchess and the Handsome Frenchman

'Will you marry me?' he asked.

As anyone who's visited Paris will know, there are two islands in the middle of the River Seine. On the bigger island, the Île de la Cité, sits the cathedral of Notre Dame. The smaller, the Île Saint-Louis, is a jewel-box of narrow streets, pretty restaurants and elegant 17th-century mansions. The islands float on the river like two barges, the bigger pulling the smaller behind it, the 'tow-rope' being a short bridge called the Pont Saint-Louis.

Standing on this bridge, you get one of the loveliest views in Paris. On one side, the buttresses of the cathedral flying out behind it like huge stone fingers. On the other, the pinnacles of the Hôtel de Ville and the tip of the Tour Saint-Jacques. The pavement cafes are crammed with people drinking coffee and brandy. Down on the river, the coal tenders navigate a path between bateaux mouches jammed with tourists. In short, it's one of the most romantic spots in the world. And there I stood, being proposed marriage by a dark, handsome Frenchman. I could hardly believe my luck.

Pierre Vandeputte-Manevy was the archetypal Gallic charmer. At twenty-six, he was three years older than me. He spoke English perfectly with a devastating French accent. He had jet-black hair

and strong, attractive features, usually wreathed in the smoke of a
Gauloises. He was certainly a ladies' man, as most Frenchmen
seemed to be, but he never tried to push his luck. Unlike the
buttoned-up British, he wore his emotions, both joy and sadness,
right on his sleeve and I found that refreshing. Above all, he was
kind, considerate and lots of fun. He also seemed to be smitten
with me, and what girl isn't flattered by that?

He was, no surprise, also a photographer and belonged to one of
the most prestigious newspaper families in Paris. His stepfather,
Raymond Manevy, was the editor of the prestigious paper *France-
Soir*, a hugely respected journalist and the author of books on the
history of the French press. Pierre, his brother Jean, and
stepbrother Alain had all followed in Raymond's footsteps, either
as journalists themselves or, in Pierre's case, as a photographer.
Even his mother, Gabrielle, had pursued a successful career as a
translator. They were a brainy lot. Obviously, there were parallels
with the so-called Spooner dynasty in London, but the
Vandeputte-Manevys were quite a lot grander. I certainly couldn't
have pictured them in Beckenham.

By the time of the scene on the Pont Saint-Louis, Pierre and I
had been courting for nearly a year. I'd often visited the elegant
Manevy apartment in the 7th arrondissement and he'd been over
to London to meet my parents.

Naturally, I'd had a fair few boyfriends before. I wasn't Lana
Turner, but I was pretty enough and boys seemed to like me. I was
certainly no shrinking violet who was shy of men. My time in
Sweden, in the USA and, above all, the *Daily Mirror* had made
sure of that. I'd had a major crush on that gorgeous older brother
when I'd been evacuated to the Clarks in Wisbech during the war.
But there had been nothing really serious, never anyone who had
made me stop and pause and wonder if he might possibly be the
one. But now there was.

Pierre always vowed that he'd fallen for me at first sight. The
French, of course, have a phrase for it – coup de foudre (a bolt of

lightning). I can't say that's what happened on my side. Maybe I was too damn British for that, but the more I saw of him, the more I liked him. Anyway, there were those six kids to be produced and, in those days, millions of girls of my age were long since mothers.

So there I stood on the Pont Saint-Louis, looking over towards Notre Dame with a delightful man offering to share his life with me. What was a girl to do? Reader, I married him.

A year or so earlier, it hadn't taken me long to pack my bags and get on that ferry. Predictably, Mum had wrung her hands, but Dad had been on my side as always.

'Go where the work is. Get more experience. You can't lose.'

My father was more than just a parent by now. He was also a professional mentor and I listened to the spirit of his advice, even if I didn't always follow it to the letter. Since I'd joined him in Fleet Street, the two of us had grown even closer, which probably wasn't easy for my mother. And now his advice was to get on that ferry.

I'd almost forgotten the beauty of Paris. I'd passed through it as a teenager with my parents on the way to summer holidays in the south, but seeing it again as an adult was a very different thing. Despite the ravages of the war, the splendour of it was, and still is, breathtaking.

In 1950, Paris was still recovering from the cancer of its Occupation by the Germans. It was only a decade since the invasion, only six years since its liberation by the Allies, when the whole city had gone mad with joy at the sight of the Americans marching down the Champs-Élysées. Many of its greatest buildings were shabby and neglected. The emotional scars of the war remained too, just under the surface. There was still deep hatred between those who had resisted the Occupation and those considered to have collaborated with it, even in the vaguest way. We'd all seen the newspaper photos of those poor shaven-headed women, demonised because they'd fraternised with German soldiers. Even great national figures like Maurice Chevalier and Coco Chanel had been criticised.

But by the time I got off the boat train at the Gare du Nord, the old Paris was coming back to life, like a widow throwing off her mourning clothes and putting on a pretty dress again. The boulevards were buzzing, the cafes and restaurants crowded and the great hotels, like the Ritz and the Meurice, reclaimed from being nests of Nazis, were crammed again with American tourists. There was still political upheaval in the wake of the war but, in the 1950s, Hollywood films like *An American in Paris* and the dazzling new fashions of Dior and Givenchy reminded the world that this had always been the city of elegance, style and seductiveness.

And there to meet me was dear Audrey Whiting. What a girl she was. At over six feet, one of the tallest women I'd ever seen. Although poised and charming, at heart she was a blunt girl from Humberside and called a spade a shovel. This was fortunate because she eventually married the *Daily Mirror*'s Editor, Jack Nener, who had the filthiest mouth imaginable. Jack was quite a short-arse and when, to the amazement of everyone, they got spliced, wags referred to them as 'Jack and the Beanstalk' or 'The Night of the Long Wives'. The surprise at these nuptials was because Audrey was generally believed to be a lesbian. Back then, I had no idea about such things at all. She was just the best mate you could hope to have. Audrey was cool. Even her disasters had style. When she crashed her car in the Rue Saint-Honoré, she went straight through a jeweller's window, which meant that the wreck was covered in diamonds.

The *Daily Mirror* hadn't given Audrey her own staff photographer in Paris so she was forced to use freelancers. These usually came from Keystone (the Paris branch of which was headed by dear old Bert Garai's brother) or, more prestigiously, the new Magnum agency set up by among others the great Henri Cartier-Bresson and Robert Capa, those two old friends of my

Dad. Audrey hadn't been here long but, typically, seemed to know everyone already. Life with Audrey and her gang was a laugh. We'd hang out in the bars and cafes, gossiping about the big stories going around and the jobs we'd either got or would like to get. There were plenty of other foreigners around, so my dodgy French didn't matter too much.

One day Audrey and I went into the Keystone office on the Rue Royale. Among the photographers milling around was a young man I hadn't seen before. Audrey's eyes lit up.

'At last! Where have you been lately? Away on a job? Come and meet my friend from London.'

I gazed at this handsome face and saw the practised charm being switched on for my benefit.

'Doreen Spooner, meet Pierre Vandeputte-Manevy. And don't be put off by the name.'

And that, essentially, was that. There were a few evenings in the bars with the gang, then I was invited out to dinner in some little bistro, just the two of us. Soon there were walks through the Tuileries Gardens and along the banks of the river in the moonlight. The usual romantic stuff, but none the less powerful for that.

As well as being highly attractive, Pierre was a talented man. He had studied art at L'École des Beaux-Arts, the alma mater of many of the greatest French painters, sculptors, architects and designers. All his life Pierre would draw beautifully, but photography was his passion.

His childhood and early life had not been easy. He was only half-French. His mother, Gabrielle, had married a Belgian called Louis Vandeputte and given birth to two sons in Brussels, Pierre and his older brother, Jean. But their father had proved to be a womaniser and a gambler, so Gabrielle had divorced him and fled home to Paris with her children, cutting off all contact with her first husband and his family. Later she married Raymond Manevy, who brought the boys up as his own. Pierre was close to his stepfather, even taking on his name, but losing his real father must have deprived him of some part of himself.

This was a particular shame because his mother was far from easy. 'Mègaby', as she was known in the family, was a real tough cookie, a domestic tyrant who liked to be in charge. I'd already discovered that Parisian women could be really snooty and Gabrielle was certainly one of those. She dressed beautifully, loved being married to a well-known figure and living in considerable style. Apart from the Paris flat, they owned not one but two houses in the country. Visiting their apartment in the Rue de la Planche, near Les Invalides, stuffed with antiques and objets d'art, was like stepping back into the past. In a sense, she lived out of her time. She would have made the perfect hostess of a literary salon in the days before the Revolution. She was a clever woman and liked you to know it. She certainly didn't like being contradicted. She couldn't half start a row. All through their lives, she and Pierre fought like cat and dog. As a boy, he'd rarely been hugged or kissed, and she locked him in a cupboard whenever he challenged her. When he grew up, she simply used the lash of her tongue. Eventually, I learned not to let it upset me, but it did at first.

Pierre's somewhat disturbed and volatile childhood was traumatised even further as a teenager. He was only sixteen when the Germans had invaded Paris and the world he knew had come tumbling down. I soon discovered that he didn't much like to talk about the war. A curtain would come down across the handsome face. Pierre, his brothers and his stepfather, Raymond, had all been in the Resistance, producing one of the underground newspapers that had been a vital means for all the different cells to keep in touch with one another. It was dangerous work. And life was hard, even for well-heeled families like the Manevys. They had often brought back the food they grew at their country home to help feed their friends in Paris, where supplies were short. I found out later that Pierre had seen some awful things – though he never spoke of them to me – the worst being in a Metro station when a friend was shot by the Gestapo in front of his eyes.

When the war was over, the promising young photographer had been commissioned by the newspaper *Le Figaro* to take photographs at the Nuremberg Trials, where the surviving monsters of the Third Reich were brought to justice. The photographs he took in Germany, of desolate figures in foggy, bomb-shattered streets, were among the best work he ever did. Sadly, Pierre was one of those many French people who were never quite able to forgive Germany. The experience of the Occupation simply cut too deep. Years later in London, when we had several German girls as au pairs, he was his usual charming self to them, but no German boyfriend was ever allowed through the door.

When Pierre and I met everything was going well for him. His reputation as a photographer was rising. He'd done some lovely shots of the film star Rita Hayworth when she'd visited Paris. He'd asked the goddess to write her autograph on his back – his mother had been furious at what she considered to be the ruination of a perfectly good shirt. More seriously, he'd taken an extraordinary portrait of the Nobel Prize-winning writer André Gide on his deathbed, which had won him a lot of praise, and agencies like Keystone were giving him plenty of commissions.

Certainly more than I was getting. Though Audrey had been throwing me as much work as she could, the jobs were not as plentiful as I'd hoped. But at least, as Dad had prophesied, I was learning more about my trade. I soon became a well-known face around both Keystone and Magnum, always hoping to be in the right place at the right time. The atmosphere at Magnum especially was truly inspirational. As I've said, this classy new picture agency had been set up by, among others, those two giants Henri Cartier-Bresson and Robert Capa.

Cartier-Bresson was the father of what is now called photojournalism or 'street' photography. He was a quiet, frail-looking man. In a crowd you'd never notice him, which was exactly the way he wanted it. He walked around with his beloved Leica 35mm, primed and ready, half-hidden under his coat. He'd even covered the silvery bits of the camera with black tape, so the light wouldn't catch it and give him away. He was as cool as a prowling cat till the moment he saw the image he wanted, then he moved with the speed of a hawk spotting its prey. He just pulled on a wire attached to the camera and captured it. People as they really were, not primped and polished in a studio. Like Pierre, as a young man he had studied painting, but changed to photography when 'I suddenly understood that a photograph could fix eternity in an instant.' He was away on assignment for months at a time, often in India and China, so I didn't see a lot of him, but once he let me shadow him out on the street to watch him at work. For a young photographer, it felt a bit like a lesson from Michelangelo.

As a personality, Robert Capa was a total contrast. One of the greatest war photographers ever, Capa was a slightly mad Hungarian. Women found him very attractive. He'd had an affair with Ingrid Bergman during the war. His other weakness was gambling. He'd put one of his expensive cameras on a table and place a bet with it. Incredibly, he never lost. Capa's life was lived out of a suitcase, going from one field of conflict to another. Not long after I knew him in Paris, he went off to one war too many, stepped on a landmine and was blown up. A huge tragedy, but he left behind him some of the most powerful images of war ever made, easily the equivalent of the great military paintings by the artists of earlier centuries. His photographs of the D-Day landings, taken under constant fire on Omaha Beach, have never been surpassed.

I couldn't wait to see the pictures these two men brought back to the Magnum office in Paris. They were never less than object lessons in photographic art. In those times, film speeds were very much slower and, right after the war, film was rationed too. You could only take five or six shots plus two or three flash-bulbs on any job. So the craft demanded was far greater than it is today. If anything, these limitations only sharpened the talent of men like Cartier-Bresson and Capa. They both had the most fantastic 'eye'. The sort of eye you're born with. I prayed that I had it too.

I'd also become addicted to the magazines in which such magical imagery appeared. Apart from Cartier-Bresson and Capa, I scoured the pages of Britain's *Picture Post* for the work of the genius Bert Hardy and of the American *Life* to try and learn from the brilliance of Andreas Feininger. I was living in a golden age of press photography and I knew it. My road-to-Damascus moment in Lapland had not been an illusion. By now, I knew that the job I did was an amazing passport, giving me access to life in all its triumphs and tragedies, wisdom and silliness, hope and despair. If my pictures could sometimes illuminate any of that, however slightly, it'd be a job worth doing. If only the bloody jobs would start coming in.

Back in London, my father had moved from the *Daily Herald* and was now editor of *Illustrated* magazine. Suddenly he landed a couple of fish for me. Very big fish indeed.

The first one was currently swimming down in the south of France. In 1951, the ex-King Edward VIII, now Duke of Windsor, published a book called *A King's Story*. Not simply a conventional autobiography but also an explanation of why he had abdicated the throne for Mrs Wallis Simpson. It was the first time he had spoken publicly about his private feelings since that famous radio broadcast in December 1936. It was sure to sell like the proverbial hotcakes but, like any author both then and now, he had to promote it. Selected reporters and photographers were to be let into the beautiful house in Biarritz where he and the Duchess were now ensconced. Since I was mostly living in Paris, I got the gig. Sheer nepotism. Shocking, really. Oh well.

When I got to Biarritz and was ushered into the royal presence, it was so hard to see why a king had abdicated his throne for that woman. Of course, that's what half the world had always said, but seeing her up close just reinforced that feeling. I didn't take to her at all. The shots were taken out in the garden of the villa. As with so many photographs taken of them, the couple seemed to have an agenda of showing how blissfully happy they were and that the crisis that rocked the monarchy had all been 'worth it'. The ex-King Edward VIII, though quite formal in manner, was pleasant and willing to please, but the ex-Mrs Simpson wasn't. She was brittle, angular, devoid of all warmth. She smiled for the camera, but like a robot. There was no feeling behind it. Only if my lens got too close, did she suddenly become animated, panicking in case it revealed the lines on her fifty-four-year-old face. When I'd finished, the Duke called to their little lapdog.

'Come on, Tom-Tom, walkies!'

'Don't call him that!' snapped the Duchess fiercely. 'His name is Thomas.'

It seemed to me that the Duchess had two lapdogs, one of whom had given up everything for her. Was this his reward? And what sort of silly cow calls her dog 'Thomas'?

Then Dad came up with a second royal gig, this one even more prestigious. To photograph Princess Elizabeth in her uniform for Trooping the Colour, a service she was about to perform on behalf of her father, King George VI, who was in poor health. I went a bit nervously to Clarence House, where she lived with Prince Philip before she came to the throne. Princess Elizabeth came outside and got onto a waiting horse. She looked, as she still does, totally natural on a horse. She was so young then, the military uniform only emphasising how beautiful she was. When she laid eyes on me, she seemed highly amused.

'Goodness, a woman photographer,' said the inimitable voice. Then to her lady-in-waiting: 'Do take a picture of her taking a picture of me.'

To my surprise, the lady produced a camera from under her jumper and did as she was ordered. Sadly, I never got to see the result. Presumably it rests inside one of Her Majesty's thousands of albums. A while back, my son-in-law contacted Buckingham

PICTURES OF A GIRL

A young Doreen captured on camera by her father Len (above) and by his friend – and her early mentor – the great Swedish photographer Karl Gullers (right)

LIFE THROUGH A LENS

Doreen the professional photographer (left): always looking for "the picture", not just the photograph. On holidays (below) with the father who first gave her a camera, and the mother who was so often troubled about the places it would take her

LOVE AND MARRIAGE

Anti-clockwise from top: Doreen (far right, on Audrey
Whiting's shoulders) and Pierre (crouching) in their
carefree early days in Paris; their "wonderful wedding"
at St Bride's church, Fleet Street, in 1952; the couple
with Anthony, Jeanne and baby Catherine – and
(above) with Pierre's mother Mègaby and the children
in France

Focusing on the very old through to the very young: the top-hatted George Bernard Shaw peering through his garden gate (left) won Doreen 'British News Picture of the Year', while his wrinkles just made Albert Einstein (opposite) more photogenic; the future King of Sweden (below) was a delightful, if fidgety, subject

Picture Post, February 15, 1947

WATERSHED MOMENT

It was Doreen's trip to Lapland, and taking the photographs of the Sami Reindeer Round-up that were printed in *Picture Post* and convinced her photography was to be her life

The Scene That Warms the Cockles of a Laplander's Heart
One trapper. Two reindeer. Three minutes' work, and £14 in the kitty.
The scene is at the annual reindeer round-up in Haerjedalen, Sweden.

Off-the-ration Sunday Dinners on the Hoof
This year, 3,000 reindeer will be killed at the round-up. Their flesh makes
good steak, their hide warm coats.

REINDEER ROUND-UP

WHAT does a Lapp dream of, as he snuggles in his furs in the long Arctic nights? He dreams of the sweet generous eyes of the reindeer, for the reindeer means riches. The big round-up takes place each January in the Haerjedalen province of Northern Sweden. As many as 3,000 reindeer are rounded-up and slaughtered.

Lapps, no fools when it comes to bargaining, negotiate the price with dealers before the kill. Last year, gnome-like little reindeer king Lars Kreik sold five hundred head for £7 apiece. Then he retired, with little more to do than dream of this year's round-up, when he hopes to break his own record. Happy Lapp! Happy dreams!

Reindeer Head and Reindeer Dead
Trapper's name is Jan Renhufvud ('reindeer head,' in English).
The dead bull reindeer is worth £7 to him.

AMERICANA 1950

Leaving a job at the Daily Mirror to take a photographic trip across America was a big risk – but produced some of Doreen's greatest pictures. Young boys play cowboy (above) outside the 'Helldorado' in Tombstone, Arizona. In Reno, Nevada (left), signs warn gamblers to risk only what they can afford – while assuring them it's a "cinch"

1950 - OR 1850?

Doreen was shocked by the working conditions, still, of black people picking cotton in Mississippi (left). The buttons on this Amish boy's dungarees (below) were only a recent innovation at the anti-modern religious community in Lancaster, Pennsylvania

PORTRAIT OF A MARRIAGE

In 1936 their romance rocked a nation. Fifteen years later, Doreen found
the now-Duchess of Windsor 'brittle, angular, devoid of all warmth. She
smiled for the camera, but like a robot'

Palace to see if they could track it down. They were very polite but
I reckon they had far better things to do with their time, like
organising a Diamond Jubilee. Never mind. Not many people can
say they've had their picture taken by personal command of the
future Queen Elizabeth II.

Less than a year later, King George VI died suddenly and the
young princess became queen. Newspapers and magazines
around the world were clamouring for pictures and the ones I'd
taken the previous summer appeared in *Newsweek* and
Cosmopolitan (precursor to today's *Cosmo*) in the USA. The
pictures were also used by BBC television before close-down
every night against the soundtrack of the national anthem. Nice
to think that the last thing the nation saw before it went to sleep
was a Doreen Spooner photograph.

I also covered the funeral of her father, that sad cortège winding
its way through streets crammed with silent crowds. He had died
too young, worn out by carrying the awful burden passed to him
by the older brother who had only cared for that vain, brittle
woman with the dog called Thomas.

So, for around a year, I commuted between London and Paris,
going wherever the work might be. This didn't seem to daunt my
ardent suitor. In those days, you could fly across the Channel for
about twenty quid and Pierre popped over several times to stay in
Beckenham. It was a comfortable but fairly ordinary house,
certainly not comparable to the splendour of his parents'
apartment in the Rue de la Planche, but he didn't seem to notice.
Dad liked him at once and he turned on the full French charm for
my mother, though she was in a tizz at the mere possibility of my
living permanently abroad. Naturally, we had separate bedrooms.
Back then, anything else would have been quite unthinkable. And
I knew that Mum was lying in bed wide awake listening for the
faintest creak on the landing.

Back in Paris, I'd moved out of Audrey's flat and found myself
a bedsit in the large house of an elderly couple near the Arc de

Triomphe. It wasn't cheap, but it was classy. By now, I was a fairly frequent guest for lunch at the Rue de la Planche. Every Saturday, Pierre's mother held an 'open house' for any family member who cared to come. Mègaby ruled the table with an iron fist that wasn't always in a velvet glove. Usually, there was a lot of arm-waving and Gallic emotion flying through the air, frequently about nothing at all. I was always expecting a few plates to fly too, but that never quite happened. The Manevys were certainly posher than the Spooners but, I soon realised, not necessarily more contented.

Pierre's stepfather, Raymond, the famous journalist, was a delight. I loved him at once and admired him just as much. I can still see him dwarfed behind his huge desk, puffing away on his pipe as he studied some heavy book.

'Ah, voici ma petite Doreen!' he'd say, a broad smile on his face, his arms thrown wide to kiss me on both cheeks.

But, not unlike the situation in Beckenham, it was the lady of the house who was the problem. Though, while my own poor Mum had very little self-esteem, Mègaby had almost too much. She didn't like her authority to be challenged and, if it was, the fireworks started. Thankfully, Mègaby seemed to like me well enough. At first, we'd stalked around each other for a while, then the relationship was mostly fine. I'm sure it helped that I was in the family business too. I think she admired me for trying to make my way in the newspaper world, just as male-dominated in France as it was in England. Maybe she also sensed that I wasn't some meek girl she could wrap around her little finger. Anyway, I'd certainly not succeeded in distancing myself from the influence of my own mother only to fall under the thumb of somebody else's.

Despite, maybe even because of, the frequent fireworks, I loved these lunches in the Rue de la Planche. Just as, when a girl, I'd liked being in the rowdy household of my cousins in north London. It felt good to be a part of the big family gathered round Mègaby's elegant table. How much more fun it was than to be an only child. All these different people coming and going, finding out about their lives, exploring the possibility of friendship.

By a stroke of luck, Pierre's older brother Jean had married another English girl called Renee, who I liked at once. When the French conversation defeated me, she and I could cling together in the face of Mègaby and talk about home. For some reason, her little boy became devoted to me and always insisted on sitting beside me. After lunch, I'd maybe take him out to the Galeries Lafayette to look at the toys. I enjoyed being somebody's almost-auntie and it stirred up that deep, eternal need to have my own children. One day soon I wanted to be a gentler, cosier version of Mègaby, at the head of my own noisy, cheery table, surrounded by people I loved and who loved me in return.

As Pierre and I grew fonder of each other and the notion of marriage, though not yet spoken aloud, entered both our minds, I asked myself if I could really envisage a permanent life away from home and the roots that had made me.

With the blind optimism of youth, the answer was 'yes'. And when, on that bridge overlooking the Seine, the question was finally popped, the answer was 'yes' again.

Chapter Six

A Tale of Two Cities

From the window of the flat, I looked out over the Left Bank of Paris. High-pitched rooftops, church spires and the turrets of the University. From the street below, I could hear the shouts of the market traders and the bicycle bells of the students whizzing past on their way to lectures. The aroma of coffee beans wafted up from the shop on the ground floor.

The first year of the marriage of Doreen Spooner and Pierre Vandeputte-Manevy was as romantic as anything could possibly be. It was like being in a slightly corny movie script. Simple English girl goes to Paris, marries handsome Frenchman, gradually loosens her British corsets and embraces the Bohemian lifestyle. She mixes with bearded, artistic types who live in paint-spattered studios with voluptuous ladies to whom they aren't married. She runs up the stairs laden with armfuls of French bread and bags of onions bought from a chap wearing a black beret and a T-shirt with horizontal stripes. Her attempts at speaking French are met with indulgent laughter by the local shopkeepers. In the movie, I'd be played by Jean Simmons or Deborah Kerr.

And that's the way it really was. The small rented apartment in the Rue de l'Estrapade where we began our life together was a gem. A pretty sitting-room with a tiny dining-room leading off it. One bedroom. Bathroom and kitchen. On the third floor. No lift. That was all. But oodles of charm. An enchanted place that had last been occupied by a famous film actress, which gave it an extra glamour.

It was in the Latin Quarter, close to the Sorbonne and to the Panthéon, the burial place of many French heroes. An area full of life, day and night. Close by on the Place de la Contrescarpe was a wonderful street market. I was soon well-known to everyone there, struggling in my basic French to buy what I needed.

'Ah, la petite Anglaise!' they'd say. If they ripped me off in any way, at least they were charming about it.

It was the perfect spot to live. Friends like Audrey Whiting and the gang from Keystone and Magnum would come over for dinner, or we'd go out to one of the cheap student restaurants that infested the narrow streets of the 5th arrondissement. On nice days, Pierre and I could take a stroll in the Jardin du Luxembourg, one of the loveliest gardens in the world, sit in the sun eating ice cream or watching the children sail their boats in the pond. In those early months it seemed as if we were living a charmed life. Maybe not Cinderella and the Prince, but pretty bloody close. I was blissfully happy.

We had been married on August 30, 1952, at St Bride's Church, Fleet Street, the 'parish church' of the newspaper industry. Designed by Sir Christopher Wren, it was a setting of extraordinary history. The poets Milton and Dryden and the diarist Samuel Pepys had all worshipped here. The interior had been gutted by fire during the Blitz but, like St Paul's Cathedral itself, it had survived, and its restoration was being paid for by the journalists and photographers of Fleet Street. Its indestructibility made it an appropriate place for us to vow to stay together for richer or poorer, for better or worse. It was a wonderful wedding. No bride could have asked for more. When I came out of the church, I was the proud Mrs Pierre Vandeputte, which is the legal name I retain to this day (Pierre had decided to drop the Manevy bit, except in his professional life).

On some strange impulse, I made Pierre walk a little way along Fleet Street before jumping into the car taking us to the reception. I suppose I was trying to show him Spooner 'territory', to help him get a sense of where I came from. The symbolism wasn't misplaced. This long narrow finger of a street, leading up the hill to St Paul's Cathedral, would be the backdrop to both our lives for many years to come, the scene of great happiness but of much sadness too.

It was a lovely wedding, a joyous day. All the extended English and French families came. Everybody, thank God, seemed to get along well. Dad and Pierre's stepfather had a lot in common, but heaven knows what Mum thought of Mègaby or vice versa. At least there were no punch-ups, no old uncle got pissed and brought up Agincourt or Waterloo or reminded the French how recently we'd liberated them from the yoke of the Nazis. Dad had splashed out on a posh 'do' at banqueting rooms in Park Lane, Mayfair, and we spent our wedding night in the Dorchester. Even Mègaby with her two country houses in the Limousin and Burgundy regions must have felt that Pierre hadn't married too far beneath him.

Mum cried a lot, of course. She knew she'd 'lost' me quite a while ago, but this put the formal seal on it. She'd have far preferred me to have married some local lad, moved into a house a few streets away, given up some crappy secretarial job and had babies. In short, to have made the choices she had made or, to be precise, the ones which had been made for her.

The honeymoon was in Positano on the Amalfi Coast. The weather perfect, the scenery spectacular. In 1952, far fewer people travelled abroad. The age of cheap air travel hadn't yet arrived. I don't remember where my parents had honeymooned but I don't expect it was anywhere more exotic than Eastbourne or Great Yarmouth. But, due to our work, Pierre and I were already well-travelled, quite sophisticated for our age. We were far from rich but we had a few bob in the bank and both sets of parents were generous. As we stood on the balcony of the Hotel Savoy and looked out towards the island of Capri, the sun seemed to be shining in every sense. We were young. We were talented. We were in love. What could possibly go wrong?

Marriage is often referred to as a 'settling-down'. Wild oats have been sown, the path we want to follow in life is becoming clearer. For the new Monsieur and Madame Vandeputte, it wasn't going to be like that at all. For the next eight years, things would be unsettled and uncertain. A tale of two cities. We'd hop to and fro between Paris and London, both for work and for family reasons. Never quite sure of the best place to be or the direction to take. These were the years when the seeds were planted that were going to cause so much heartbreak later.

But at first, in our little eyrie in the Rue de l'Estrapade, everything was wonderful. The honest truth was that we'd moved into it a while before the wedding, a fact that, had she known it, would have caused my Mum to drop dead with shock (the sexual revolution was still a decade off).

Just before we'd got married Pierre had landed a really good job at *Le Figaro*, one of France's most important newspapers. He was to be Picture Editor, the same job that my Dad and Uncle Frank did in London. It was a big feather in the cap of a twenty-eight-year-old photographer. In the event it didn't work out so well. As I explained before, Picture Editors don't themselves take photographs. They're in charge of evaluating and selecting the work of other people. Soon Pierre missed creating his own work and the hurly-burly of the streets. We'd sit in a bar with our photographer friends hearing what they'd done that day and I could see that he was envious. And *Le Figaro* was quite a 'heavy' paper, the French equivalent of the *Daily Telegraph* in Britain. What Pierre most enjoyed was lighter stuff, glamorous even. Film stars, pop singers, the whirligig of showbiz. Maybe it was a reaction against the seriousness of his stepfather's journalism. Maybe just a way of forgetting the things he'd seen during and after the war.

I was still doing some jobs via the picture agencies and for Audrey Whiting on the *Daily Mirror*. During this time, I covered the visit of the young Princess Margaret to Paris and photographed her with General Eisenhower and, more to her taste I suspect, with Christian Dior, the Parisian designer who had revolutionised fashion after the war with his 'New Look' which quickly swept the world. The young Margaret was certainly model material. She looked wonderful in those full, flowing Dior skirts. At this point in time, soon after the death of King George VI, she was adjusting to being no longer the daughter of the King, merely the sister of the Queen. Searching for a new role, she decided to fall in love and would soon trigger a crisis almost in the league of the one created by her 'wicked' uncle, Edward VIII. Because photographers, like portrait painters, spend so much time looking at faces, they can become quite sharp judges of character. I could see that the pretty, self-assured Margaret was a very different kettle of fish from her more reserved, conventional sister. Though she conscientiously performed her often-dull official engagements, I felt that Margaret was just longing to kick off her shoes, light up a fag and pour herself a stiff gin.

Another group of princesses were the Bluebell Girls, the world-famous troupe of showgirls based at the famous Lido cabaret on the Champs-Élysées. Nearly all the girls were pushing six-foot tall, and with their staggeringly high heels and feathered headdresses looked like gorgeous giantesses on the stage, towering over international stars like Édith Piaf, Noël Coward and Marlene Dietrich. The creator of the troupe was Margaret Kelly, an Irish girl who'd risen from near-poverty in Britain to being one of the most iconic women in France, eventually winning the Légion d'Honneur. I lined up a few Bluebells near the Eiffel Tower but put Kelly, known as Miss Bluebell, right at the front in star position where she truly belonged. At the age of at least fifty, she could do a high-kick as well as any of them. Behind the sequins, the champagne and the stage-door admirers, it was a demanding life and a short career. In one of my favourite pictures, I snapped a showgirl in the dressing-room at the Lido, after yet another exhausting show, her aching feet up on the dressing table. Not unlike my fantasy of Princess Margaret really. Just two young girls doing very different but equally tough jobs.

For that first year of my marriage, I was having a lot of fun being a photographer in the most beautiful city in the world. I had a social life with clever and buzzy people, was part of the big bustling family that gathered around Mègaby's table every Saturday, with enough money to pay the rent. And a husband who loved me.

But the idyll was short-lived. One morning, I was sick. Really sick. Two and two were soon put together and the doctor confirmed it. It hadn't been planned but it was nevertheless a huge joy. As I got bigger, the news spread fast around the street and the marketplace.

'La petite Anglaise est enceinte!'

'Madame Vandeputte? Non!'

'C'est vrai!'

'Merveilleux!'

Everybody seemed to be pleased. My parents were thrilled to bits. Even Mègaby, hardly the most maternal of women, hadn't flinched at the prospect of being a grandmother again. I just prayed that my waters wouldn't break during lunch in the Rue de la Planche, all over the Aubusson carpet.

Though I was young and healthy, it was hard not to worry a little. That empty cradle beside my mother's hospital bed still haunted me. But I knew it was simply a matter of luck. What would be, would be. It helped that I'd already seen childbirth close up. In a town called Chelles just outside Paris was a doctor who was loved and trusted by everyone there. But he was a blind man who diagnosed illnesses largely by touch. He had delivered over two thousand babies the same way and I had been allowed to photograph one such birth. Watching this man bring a life into the world with such incredible gentleness and skill had been an extraordinary sight. More than ever, I wanted to have a child myself.

But I soon realised that being 'enceinte' wasn't always a million laughs. The three flights of stairs to our love-nest, up which I'd previously scampered with my shopping, gradually turned into Mount Everest. It would have been nice if all the people who were so delighted at my condition had helped me up those stairs with the groceries. Soon my work had to stop too. Running around the streets of Paris with a camera in one hand and a heavy bag full of lenses and flash-guns in the other was no longer a great idea.

But all went well and, after nine months, Anthony Vandeputte was born. Pierre, always an emotional man, was beside himself with pride at having a son. The two families cracked open bottles of champagne. And me? Did that experience I had always longed for, the miracle of bringing another human being into the world, live up to expectations? Oh yes. Without a doubt. One down, five more to go.

Of course a baby changes everything. Our flat in the Latin Quarter became somewhat less romantic. The delicious scent that drifted up from the coffee shop was soon defeated by rather less appealing smells. In bed at night, I no longer listened to the bells of the nearby church tolling the hours, but to the wailing of a hungry infant. Nappies, washed by hand in the sink, hung dripping above the bath. It wasn't long before hauling the baby in his carry-cot up and down those stairs became no fun at all. It was clear that our days in the Rue de l'Estrapade were numbered.

Just at the right moment, another small miracle occurred. At least it seemed so. Pierre was poached from *Le Figaro* and offered the job of London-based photographer for a new French magazine. Tired of being stuck behind the picture desk and itching to get back onto the streets, he leapt at it. I was thrilled too. Despite my love of Paris and our life there, I felt it was just the right moment. Audrey Whiting had recently left to run the New York office of the *Daily Mirror* and I missed her a lot. Since I'd given birth, I'd seen less of my other friends too. With Pierre at work, my only company was the baby, my only outings pushing the pram along the Boulevard Saint-Michel to look at the shops or to the Jardin du Luxembourg to look at the ducks. It's amazing how fast shops and ducks can get boring. Our beloved little flat sometimes felt like a gilded cage. These emotions were familiar to millions of new mothers from that day to this, however much they love their child.

So we went home. My Dad helped us to buy a house in Beckenham, not far from him and Mum. It was wonderful to have more space in which to bring up a baby, though the dozy avenues of Beckenham didn't quite have the elegance or the buzz of the Latin Quarter.

But at least Britain seemed cheerier than it had been when I'd set off on my travels. It was the 'New Elizabethan Age'. The princess who'd had my picture taken in the grounds of Clarence House was now on the throne. There had been a surge of optimism that the long shadow of the war could finally be put behind us. Rationing was over, more people had this amazing new gadget called a television set and the earliest sounds of rock and roll were beginning to drift across the ocean from the USA.

Sadly, the Labour Party, still under the ageing Clement Attlee, lost the election to the Conservatives under their sexy new leader, Anthony Eden. The Labour-supporting *Daily Mirror* had screamed, 'Don't let the Tories cheat our children!', but it hadn't been enough. At least that old bulldog Winston Churchill had finally retired. I'd done some good pictures of him back in Paris but Pierre had taken a sheaf of even better ones in London, which had cheesed me off a bit. What a face the old man had. A photographer's dream, just like Albert Einstein. But however admired he still was, his was a face from the past and people wanted new heroes.

In Beckenham, my mother was ecstatic at having both her daughter and her new grandchild within easy reach. And soon I was 'enceinte' again. Our daughter Jeanne was born in 1955. Two down, four to go.

Pierre was doing a lot of good work. He loved all the showbiz stars, the theatrical first nights, the movie premieres. He did wonderful shots of celebrities such as Laurence Olivier and Vivien Leigh, Noël Coward, Elizabeth Taylor and Mike Todd, Bette Davis, Margot Fonteyn and Orson Welles. And an especially fine series of a grey-haired Charlie Chaplin wandering the streets of London where he'd spent his youth. During the great hoo-ha over Princess Margaret's desire to marry Group Captain Peter Townsend, Pierre got quite chummy with the princess's sweetheart as he pursued him all over London, hoping for that one 'picture' that would tell the nation everything it needed to know.

Despite all this and the fun of his first daughter, Pierre sometimes appeared to be less than completely happy. These were like distant rumbles of thunder and the smile would soon come out again. But the rumbles became more frequent and when I finally asked him, he confessed that he didn't much like the people he was working for and wanted to leave. He'd been asking around London and there was a job going as a Paris photographer for the *Daily Mail*.

'What do you think?' he asked me.

'It's what you really want?' I replied, trying not to show that my heart had sunk to my boots.

'Only if you'd be happy too.'

'I'll be fine,' I replied.

Mum and Dad were sad but stoical. It was our lives, they said. But I'd imagine my mother took to her bed on quite a few afternoons. She doted on her grandchildren. They had brought new light into her overshadowed life. But the house was sold, my father repaid and the White Cliffs of Dover vanished behind us in the mist.

In Paris, it felt like we'd never been away. Back we went to the Saturday lunches in the Rue de la Planche. Back we went on our regular visits to Mègaby in the country. Back Pierre went to being a Frenchman. He was like a duck who'd wandered off somewhere, sliding back into the waters of his own pond with a sigh of pleasure.

Now we had two young kids, a trendy flat in central Paris wasn't an option. A house was found in Bois-Colombes, a pretty suburb a couple of miles north of the Arc de Triomphe. Pierre's new job paid well and it was a fine house, three storeys high, with a big garden for the children. It was easily the grandest place I'd lived in. The rooms were large and a splendid wooden staircase curved up from the elegant hall. Even Mègaby, who arrived on her first visit more than ready to sniff at our suburban villa, had trouble finding anything to sniff about.

There was a big cellar too, entered by an archway over which my husband painted 'Pierre's Bistro'. Here he created what we'd now call a man-cave, a little bar with sofas and tables. Anyone visiting for dinner would first have a drink down there. It was all very chic, very French. Not the sort of thing you'd find in Beckenham. Pierre was a wonderful host. The glasses were always well filled.

Tony, aged four and quite a handful, went to the local primary school and was already becoming bi-lingual, as baby Jeanne eventually would too. It was now that I got the first in a long series of au pairs to help with the baby and running this large house. Her name was Rosemary, a German girl who'd come to Paris to learn the language. We gave her board, lodging and a small wage and she gave me an extra pair of hands during the day, going to her language school in the evenings. It worked perfectly. The kids adored her and vice versa.

Above all, she gave me a little freedom. The children were

everything to me, but I'd have been lying if I'd said I never missed my work. Sometimes, doing the chores or feeding the baby in the sunny garden, I'd see myself on those skis in Lapland, Albert Einstein's grumpy face or Princess Elizabeth and my photograph in the gardens of Clarence House. I'd wonder where Cartier-Bresson was and what amazing things he was doing. I'd think back to the photographer's room in the *Daily Mirror*, all of them standing there with the cake they'd bought me after I'd passed their tests. 'Welcome aboard, Doreen.'

In the evening, when the kids were in bed and Rosemary had gone off to her language school, the big house could seem quite lonely. Pierre might not be back till late; maybe still on a job but more likely in some bar in town with his mates. He'd be in that smoky, stimulating world I'd once inhabited myself, but from which I was now cut off. But the advent of Rosemary gave me the chance to stick my nose back in.

Through Magnum and Keystone, I began to do some little jobs. The Hollywood film star Edward G Robinson, most famous for his gangster roles, had a face almost as great as Einstein's. So did Charles Laughton, star of *The Hunchback of Notre Dame* and many other classics. Poor Laughton believed himself to be hideously ugly but, to a photographer, there was real beauty in that face. And so, in a very small way, I kept in practice. Then it was back to the house in Bois-Colombes and being Madame Vandeputte.

Pierre was happy in his new job and life went on. I got pregnant again and, in 1959, Catherine was born. Dark in looks like her brother and sister, she seemed to take after Pierre's side rather than mine, a fact that pleased Mègaby no end. Clearly the Vandeputte gene pool was as dominating as my mother-in-law herself. Three down, three to go. I'd have to hurry. I was thirty-one now and by the standards of the time my clock was ticking fast.

By the time of Catherine's birth, it was nearly a decade since I'd picked up the phone on that bored, aimless morning and called Audrey Whiting in Paris. That casual call had brought me great fun, fascinating work, treasured friendships and, above all, a dear and loving husband and three adored kids. I had a lovely home, no money worries and good health. I had no grounds whatever for complaint.

And yet something about my life didn't fit. It rubbed up against me like a badly fitting shoe. Weighed against all my advantages, it seemed trivial, ungrateful even but it was there none the less and, as time passed, it became slowly more uncomfortable. What was it? Some combination of homesickness and, don't laugh, of patriotism.

We all have roots. Despite all my travels, I guess mine were stronger than I'd imagined and that I'd been denying it to myself for a long time. My short period back in London had stoked that feeling. It had felt so good to be near my parents again, not just my dear Dad but my troubled mother too. They came over to visit of course, but it wasn't the same. And they weren't getting any younger. As time had passed, I'd noticed a slight resentment of Pierre growing in my mother. He'd been the reason I'd finally left her, after all.

But there was something else. I'd never been a flag-waver, but I'd always been quietly proud of being British. Despite the gloom and hard slog of the post-war years, the map of the world was still covered in all those pink bits. We'd faced up to Hitler and, at huge cost, defeated him. When France and other countries had caved in, we'd stood firm, at one point almost alone. I'd not forgotten those cold nights in the Anderson shelter, that white shirt flapping in the branches of the tree and trying not to cry when I climbed aboard the train to be evacuated from London. We might be a small country with a lousy climate but, my God, we were bloody amazing when we needed to be. Somebody once wrote that a baby born British had won the lottery of life. It was exactly how I felt.

But my three kids were losing out on that opportunity. By now, the two older ones spoke French better than me and I wondered if a point would come when the chatter in my home would be mostly in a language that wasn't mine. So the day arrived when Pierre and I had the same conversation that had taken us back to France three years before, but this time in reverse.

'I'd really like to go home,' I said nervously.

'It's what you definitely want?'

'Only if you'll be happy too.'

'Ok, if that's what you think is best.'

Looking back, I realise now how lucky I was in my husband. Despite the fact that we were both city people with a progressive outlook, people who'd seen a fair bit of the world, the old notion that the man was head of the house and had the final say in important matters was very far from dead. Much as I'd have liked to pretend otherwise, it was far from dead in me either. But Pierre was made from finer cloth. I've already said he was a 'ladies' man' but that went much deeper than the usual meaning of that phrase. He was a perceptive human being, always sensitive to everyone else's feelings, especially those of women. Surprising really, since he'd been raised by the thick-skinned Mègaby. Or maybe that was why.

So the 'For Sale' sign went up outside the pretty house in Bois-Colombes. There was a last Saturday lunch in the Rue de la Planche. Behind his pipe, old Raymond Manevy was very sad and not looking well. If Mègaby was angry with me for taking her son and grandchildren away again she wasn't going to let me see it. The crates and the cases were packed. The older kids said goodbye to their friends at school. The bar in 'Pierre's Bistro' closed for the last time.

It was a wrench to drive away from the house where we'd been happy, but Pierre kept the usual smile on his face. If I remembered that he'd not been happy during his first brief time in England, I managed to push it to a distant corner of my mind. How selfish that was.

I glanced back at the house as it vanished around the corner.

Though we'd visit regularly to see Pierre's family, we would never live in France again. Things would never be quite the same. So it was goodbye to that magical city. To the little third-floor flat on the Rue de l'Estrapade, high up among the rooftops. To the Jardin du Luxembourg and the Boulevard Saint-Michel. To the little bridge behind Notre Dame where the handsome Frenchman had asked me to marry him. And to those first happy chapters of our life together.

Despite all that, I was jubilant as we drove away. I couldn't wait to get 'home'. I didn't realise I had just made the worst mistake of my life.

Chapter Seven

Reflections on a Mirror

He came into the kitchen with a ghost-white face, the newspaper hanging limply in his hand. He tossed it onto the breakfast table.

'How the hell did you manage that?' he asked.

'Just a lucky break.'

'But I've been after them for months.'

'Well you know how it goes. Right time, right place. Luck of the draw.'

My picture of Christine Keeler and Mandy Rice-Davies stared up at me amid the tea cups and the toast rack. 'Those two tarts' with whom the country was obsessed. And Pierre was too.

Somehow, with his French charm no doubt, he'd managed to gain Keeler's confidence and she'd even let him photograph her in her flat. They were quite sexy pictures too. The shy persona Keeler adopted as she dashed from a taxi into the Old Bailey had completely gone. The poses she'd given to my husband were flirtatious, seductive even. She'd clearly trusted him, fancied him maybe. The two older kids teased him, called her 'Dad's girlfriend' and gave him a Valentine card signed 'with lots of love from Christine'. They were good pictures, but my photograph of Keeler and Rice-Davies together, taken unawares on the first day of the trial, had far greater news value.

'You're not cross are you?' I asked.

'Why should I be?' he said, and walked out of the room. He didn't speak again for hours.

That's when I realised I had another problem. In addition to keeping the roof over our heads and trying to cope with my husband's alcoholism, now there was professional jealousy to deal with too.

There was always a bit of rivalry between press photographers, even at the *Daily Mirror*, where everyone got along so well. A scoop is a scoop after all. But it was usually mild and always matey; 'you jammy bugger', that sort of thing. In France, there had never been any tension between Pierre and me on that score. He had always admired my early work and my guts in making it in a job so dominated by men. Anyway, he'd always been the breadwinner. After our marriage and the kids were born, I'd not done much work at all. Just enough to keep my hand in.

Now though, the dynamic of our relationship had altered. Since the day the bailiff came and the truth spilled out, I'd been forced to take some control, forced to make that trembling call to the *Mirror* to see if they'd take me back after all those years. And now I was doing pretty well. The front page of that morning's paper proved it in black and white. But the caption under the photograph didn't read 'Mrs Pierre Vandeputte', it read 'Doreen Spooner'.

Pierre was an intelligent, cultured and sensitive person, as far from a 'caveman' type as it was possible to be. But he was still a man and, half a century ago, the notion of what a man should be was much more ingrained. Among many men, the concept of a wife who went out to work reflected badly on themselves. A 'real' man should earn enough to make that unnecessary. Pierre was also battling an awful addiction, as well as shame and remorse at the pain he had caused to those he loved. In short, he didn't need any more arrows piercing his self-esteem. The picture of Keeler and Rice-Davies on the front page of the *Mirror* did just that.

I reminded myself I'd had no choice but to go out to work. And to keep my job, I needed to do it as well as I could. Now it seemed the result was going to be a new cause of strain on my already bruised marriage. I felt as if I couldn't win.

That day we'd driven away from the house in Bois-Colombes was, in retrospect, the beginning of the end of my married happiness. The end of the good times.

At first, that hadn't been apparent at all. Pierre had landed a good job freelancing for the Black Star picture agency. We'd bought our nice house in Shortlands, not far from my parents, who were thrilled to have us back again. With the resilience of young children, Anthony and Jeanne had slipped easily enough into their new London primary schools. I was sure my instinct to come home had been the right one. For the next two years, I went on believing that. But I should have seen the signs.

What had happened during our brief return to London four years earlier now happened again. Uprooted from his own country, something in Pierre had begun to wither. Try as he might, he just couldn't settle. Despite loving me and his children, despite his intelligence and his talent, these just weren't strong enough to negate some sense of emptiness that had taken hold inside him. I suppose if anyone should have understood this, it ought to have been me. For heaven's sake, it was exactly the same thing that had made me drag us all back to Britain. But in getting my way, I'd just transferred that emptiness from myself to my husband.

Another factor came into it too. I've already said what a macho culture Fleet Street had always been. Testosterone Alley might have been a better name. Sadly, a part of that was xenophobia, a cancer that still infects people in Britain today but which, back then, was almost respectable. Otherwise decent people thought it was perfectly OK to talk about 'Johnny Foreigner' with prejudice and condescension. In the case of a Frenchman, there was scorn mixed in too. Hadn't we liberated the 'Frogs' during the war, because they were too feeble to do it themselves? Why was this Pierre bloke coming over here and taking a job an Englishman could have done? Not right at all, they were saying behind his back in the local pubs.

In those days, Fleet Street floated on a river of alcohol. The local watering-holes depended almost entirely on the custom of the newspapers. The main *Mirror* pub was the White Hart at the top of Fetter Lane. Hugh Cudlipp, the paper's Editorial Director, had christened it the 'Stab in the Back', because so much trouble began under its nicotine-stained roof. Its customers weren't entirely *Mirror* people, other papers used it too. So this was where gossip and rumour took hold, where affairs started and finished, where promising people were poached from one paper to another.

Most newspapers, and certainly tabloids like the *Daily Sketch* and the *Mirror*, were hugely successful, really coining it in. The one and only commercial television channel was still in its infancy, so nearly all advertising went to the popular papers and magazines. It was the age of milk and honey. There were endless long lunches, fat expense accounts. Everybody worked hard, so they played hard too. The release of booze and fags were safety valves from the pressure, which is why so many found them indispensable. And Pierre Vandeputte, trying to deal with both the job and the veiled ostracism he found there, needed that release more than most.

Many people who've been alcoholics, or who've been close to one, will say they didn't notice the tipping point where heavy social drinking went over the line into an illness. Certainly, I didn't register it happening to my husband, though when people began to have an alcohol problem, they usually realised the need to conceal it. Secretiveness and deception became new characteristics. I'd later find out from Pierre's colleagues that they'd discovered empty vodka bottles submerged in the water tanks in the newspaper's darkrooms. Of course, what he was really drowning was his career and his happy marriage.

It was only when the bailiff knocked that the truth exploded into my life. I should have seen it before, I told myself. I should have been able to stop it. But it was too late now.

That first day back at the *Daily Mirror* in 1962 had been a challenge: leaving the kids with a stranger, getting on the train into the city, standing outside the massive building at Holborn Circus. Then there was my surprise at how little had changed inside this spanking new headquarters. The smell of the newsroom was the same, the camera technology was the same, above all the attitude of the men was no different. They still assumed I'd been hired to do the typing. When given the truth, they were fine and welcoming. It was just the assumption that got up your nose.

It was a paradox though. The newspapers of Fleet Street were supposed to be the opinion formers for the 'great unwashed' to follow. In reality it was the other way around. As I've written, the early Sixties was a time of huge cultural change in Britain. Since the young Queen had come to the throne in 1952, things had certainly moved on. The Suez Crisis in 1956 had shown that we were no longer the great world power we once were. Rock and roll had come across the Atlantic and swept all before it. Now the kids worshipped Buddy Holly and Elvis Presley. In the theatre, *Look Back in Anger* had started a revolt against the drawing-room comedies of the post-war era and made playwrights like John Osborne the loud voices of a new generation.

A new age really was dawning and, in the early Sixties, it accelerated fast. It was cocky young Mandy Rice-Davies who caught the changing mood in one sentence. When told in court that the-then Lord Astor denied having had an affair with her and so, by implication, she must be lying, she just stared at the barrister and replied, 'Well he would, wouldn't he?'

Somehow it was end of deference. No peer of the realm, no posh barrister in a wig scared this girl. These young people were no longer intimidated by the power of the Establishment.

Indirectly due to the Profumo Affair, the Macmillan government foundered and, soon afterwards, Labour under Harold Wilson came to power. Instead of aristocratic Tories with their estates and grand connections, we were now led by the middle-class academic Wilson with his pipe and his Gannex raincoat. The Beatles were awarded MBEs, causing scores of retired military men to send theirs back in disgust. It really did feel like Britain might be changing.

But inside the glass towers of Fleet Street, the old macho ways still reigned supreme. Except in one particular and very important way. From the Sixties onwards, a new type of journalist emerged. The women's journalist. One by one, a parade of highly talented females appeared and would change Fleet Street forever. These included Jean Rook at the *Daily Express*, Katharine Whitehorn at *The Observer* and Marje Proops at the *Daily Mirror*. Not forgetting my old chum from Paris, the woman who'd introduced me to Pierre, the giantess Audrey Whiting.

Audrey in particular had shown just how much a clever woman journalist could contribute to the success of a newspaper. Her great coup is still mentioned in awe in newspaper circles. After Audrey left Paris, she'd been sent first to New York then back to London and married the foul-mouthed *Mirror* editor Jack Nener. Back then, Fleet Street frowned on husbands and wives working together so Audrey had gone across to the *Sunday Pictorial*. Here she followed up a story in medical journal *The Lancet* about a German woman who claimed to have given birth while still a virgin. This story doubled the *Pictorial*'s circulation and swept the world. A bit more respect was shown to women journalists after that, but nowhere near enough.

But by the time I returned to the *Mirror*, the great Marje Proops had started her forty-year career at the paper, first as a feature writer then as Britain's most famous 'agony aunt'. She was unforgettable, with her huge glasses, big nose and long cigarette holder. When she still did features, I was sometimes sent out with her on a job. Once, as we walked down the platform at Euston, the unmistakeable Marje was spotted by the train driver leaning out of his cab window.

'Bloody hell, folks, we've got Marje on board today,' he shouted to anyone who could hear. 'So everything's going to be just fine.'

And, of course, it was. That was the way she made you feel. Everybody loved Marje. I certainly did. She became a real friend and, in the rough times to come in my life, I more than once sneaked upstairs to her posh office for a shoulder to cry on and some practical advice. She never failed me.

She was a tough cookie though and didn't suffer fools gladly. She was well aware of her star status and loved every minute of it. The stars themselves adored her. She often lunched with Cary Grant, listened to Sophia Loren's woes and once threw herself at the Archbishop of Canterbury, mistaking his outstretched arms – a gesture of blessing – for a desire to have a hug.

Dear Marje would hug anyone, either in the flesh or through her column. Over the years, in one way or another, Marje reached out and embraced millions of people. She and her assistants answered tens of thousands of letters a year, both on and off the page. She never learned to type – all her columns were hand-written. And she was a bloody good writer: warm, simple, straight to people's hearts. That's why the train driver at Euston, who'd maybe never even read her column, was so glad to see her.

Marje made such a great 'agony aunt' because she had a huge, inexhaustible well of empathy inside her. Her own life hadn't been a bed of roses. She'd grown up believing she was ugly and not worth much. She'd gratefully grabbed the first man who asked her to marry him. Though she kept up the façade of a happy marriage, losing her virginity and giving birth had both been terrifying experiences. It didn't put her off men though and she had a long-term extra-marital affair with a lawyer at the *Mirror*, a secret kept from her readers, but well-known to everyone at Holborn Circus. It was a complicated life. So when Marje gave out advice, she usually knew what she was talking about.

It's no exaggeration to say that female journalists like Marje, Jean Rook and Katharine Whitehorn changed millions of people's lives, not all of them female. They wrote about the experiences of ordinary women and made them feel that their worries and woes, their dreams and aspirations, were just as important as those of men. They wrote about things that had been swept under the carpet in a buttoned-up Britain, which was then far more under the influence of the church than it is now. Not just sexual issues like contraception, abortion, pre-marital sex and infidelity, although those figured prominently ('why shouldn't a woman have a right to an orgasm?' asked Marje), but emotional ones such as self-expression, the urge to have a career and to have equality with your male partner. These were the things I was struggling with too and always would. So I lapped up these revolutionary columns as eagerly as any woman stuck at home with the kids. The place where, of course, I felt I really ought to be.

So, when I went back to work I certainly wasn't the only woman there. Upstairs was the Women's Department where the magnificent Felicity Green ruled the roost with her gang of girl assistants. But I was a bit cut off from all that. Down in the photographers' room I was still the only person wearing a dress. And old habits died hard. If somebody was needed to go and get the coffees from the miraculous new vending machines, I heard myself volunteering more often than was fair and nobody tried to stop me. On the other hand, they were fiercely protective.

'Here, you watch your language, mate. There's a lady present,' they'd say, if some interloper had used a naughty word. 'We don't swear when Doreen's around, so you don't either. Got it?'

Being a close friend of Audrey Whiting had laid me open to the suspicion in some quarters that maybe I swung both ways too. These days, nobody would give a damn, but back then my 'boys' would rise up in outrage if anyone suggested I wasn't 100 per cent red-blooded heterosexual woman. They were my knights in shining armour.

Fleet Street was a small world. Everyone gossiped about what went on at other papers. So it was well-known that the photographers at the *Mirror* got on so well (rumour had it that the photographers' room at the *Daily Express* was a nest of vipers).

'What is it with you lot?' somebody from another paper asked me once over a drink in the Stab in the Back. 'All that bleedin' sweetness and light.'

But it was true. We all respected each other. We learnt from each other. We got to know everybody's different strengths and weaknesses, and we'd help one another as much as possible if the pressure was getting heavy.

The person who needed to know us all best was Simon Clyne, the Picture Editor who'd known me, through my Dad, since I was a child and who'd given me my second chance to 'darken the *Mirror*'s door'. If anyone was responsible for the fact that we all got on so well, it was Simon. He saw his team as one big jigsaw that had to fit perfectly together, if the photographic needs of the paper were to be met. He interviewed potential new recruits several times, never hiring anyone unless he felt pretty certain they would fit in. He could be tough and authoritarian but he was a good boss. You always knew he had confidence in you because you'd not have been on his team if he hadn't. That made you always want to do your best for him. He never patronised me as a woman, never gave me only 'girly' assignments. Yes, he'd send me to a fashion show in Mayfair, but he'd also send me down a coal-mine if it suited him.

All of us were called 'staff photographers'. Strictly speaking, that meant we had to go out and shoot anything we were ordered to. From the Prime Minister in Downing Street or the Chelsea Flower Show to a strike at a factory or some awful disaster. That was the theory and it was adhered to as much as possible. In practice, however, jobs would be steered in the direction of the person who was best at that particular sort of work. It made sense both in terms of the quality delivered and helped to create a happy ship.

But it didn't always turn out that way. Poor Arthur Sidey, who specialised in photographing animals, hated it when I wasn't available and he was sent out on a fashion shoot.

'Oh, Doreen, thank God you're back,' he'd say. 'I can't bear shooting these pretty girls. I want to go back to my elephants and rhinos.'

It was always the variety that I loved. When you went in every day, you hadn't a clue what might come your way. In the photographers' room, everyone had their own locker, not just to keep your cameras safe but also a small suitcase with all the essentials for a couple of nights away, in case some big story suddenly blew up. Since I had the kids, I tried to minimise these trips, especially at weekends, but sometimes it was unavoidable. I couldn't be a part of the team and not pull my weight. Anyway, there's no denying it was rather nice to be standing on the platform at Shortlands Station in the morning and find yourself in an elegant bedroom at the Ritz in Madrid that very night. But it could just as easily be Mrs McTavish's Guest House in some village in the middle of nowhere, so it wasn't all beer and skittles. But it was nearly always interesting, challenging and sometimes even exciting. If I really had to earn a living, and I certainly did, there couldn't have been a more rewarding job.

I was lucky in that my time at the *Daily Mirror* coincided with its zenith. Beside it, the 'serious' papers looked like pygmies. There was real kudos in working for the *Mirror*. There was pride too. I'd never been terribly political, but I was pleased to be working for a left-leaning paper that had always championed ordinary, working people and which gave them a voice. In the 1960s, just as Harold Wilson's Labour was the government for the times, the *Daily Mirror* was the paper for those times.

I was one of these working people myself. The print unions were very powerful back then; too powerful really, because they could hold newspaper proprietors to ransom very easily. The tiniest dispute could shut down a paper in the blink of an eye and huge sums of money would be lost. The good side of the coin was that newspaper staff were well protected. During my first *Mirror* stint, in the late Forties, I'd been dragged reluctantly to a union meeting. Oh, how boring it had been. A lot of old blokes in shirt sleeves blustering away about bugger all. Then I'd discovered they were busy fighting to have photographers' wages almost tripled – a battle they'd won. I'd changed my mind about unions sharpish after that.

It sounds pompous, but a kind of integrity existed at the *Daily Mirror*, not always the case at other papers. There was an unspoken rule that if a reporter or photographer felt it morally wrong to do something, you could just walk away and it wouldn't count against you. Naturally, they wanted you to get scoops, but the brazen acts of some of today's paparazzi would never have been admissible. The pursuit of Princess Diana into the tunnel in Paris in which she died would have horrified all of us.

My 'boys' at the *Mirror* were a group of incredibly gifted photographers. The doyen of them all was Freddie Reed, the famous royal photographer. He was a real 'gentleman', on cosy terms with half the royal family, especially the Queen Mother, who respected him enormously. He worked at the *Mirror* for just over half a century. He lived quite close to me and would sometimes drive me home from the office. These rides down through south London and out into the suburbs were often little masterclasses in my trade. As with the mentors I'd had when I was starting out, you could learn more from Freddie's tales in half an hour than you would from any formal photographic course. It was Freddie who had spouted that essential piece of advice for every photographer, the one which had come into my head in the doorway of the ladies' loo, when I'd been struggling to capture Christine and Mandy.

'I've got lots of photographs,' he used to say in frustration. 'But

I'm not sure I've got a picture.'

Kent Gavin eventually took over Freddie's mantle. The royal family admired him just as much and soon gave him their trust, in particular Princess Diana. They knew a real pro when they saw one and 'Gavvers' was a wonderful photographer who not only took some of the best royal shots ever, but did terrific work across every other field too. His real first name was Kenneth but, on hiring him, Simon Clyne had decided that Kent was snappier, so Kent it became. Such was the power of the Picture Editor in the golden age of Fleet Street. The newly christened Kent went on to win about one-hundred-and-fifty professional awards. 'Jammy bugger' and no mistake. But they couldn't have been given to a nicer man.

As I've said, Arthur Sidey was our man for animal shots. If you wanted a photo of pandas mating, hyenas laughing or a rabbit coming out of Paul Daniels' top hat, you went to Arthur. Among his more bizarre pics were a parrot on a bike and a dog tanning himself on a sun lounger with his paws behind his head. Great stuff.

Sport was the province of Monte Fresco, the man with a name like a soft drink. In his time, Monte covered seven World Cups and over forty Cup Finals and Wimbledons. His speciality was the slightly humorous sporting picture. He liked to get something a bit quirky and off the wall. Among his most iconic shots were Vinnie Jones 'tackling' Paul Gascoigne and Dave Mackay breaking the same leg for a second time. Many of Monte's best shots ended up on T-shirts, coffee-mugs and plastered over the bedroom walls of thousands of teenage boys.

Crime stories were usually the province of Albert Foster. This was the age of the Kray brothers and other vicious East End gangs, and Albert's speciality could be dodgy work. It wasn't unknown for money to change hands in order to get a really good shot. Albert once slipped me a hundred quid too, but this was for a very different reason. For years, it lay tucked away in an envelope at the back of my locker. It was the cash to pay for the drinks at Albert's wake, just in case he had caught some gangster's 'bad' side and was suddenly despatched to that big photographic studio in the sky. Thankfully, it was never needed and I gave it back to him when I retired before he did.

The Hungarian-born Bela Zola had been at the *Mirror* since he and I had first walked in there together back in 1948. Bela was perhaps the ultimate example of the versatility expected of a staff photographer. He could do anything and always did it beautifully. Like Pierre, he'd taken great shots of The Beatles as they exploded into worldwide fame and also been badly affected by what he'd seen during the Aberfan disaster. Bela had also taken one of the most memorable press shots of the Fifties, when he'd shot a row of Teddy boys in their Sunday suits trying to sing hymns in a church. For many people, Teddy boys were the personification of evil, the reason why modern Britain was 'going to the dogs'. Bela's poignant shot showed them for what they really were, just little lads who liked to outrage the older generation. It was one of the great 'pictures'.

Though the photographers' room at the *Mirror* was supposed to be fairly democratic, there was an unspoken pecking order. I certainly wasn't at the top, as I wasn't at the top in the salary stakes either. But that was fine by me. When I'd joined the paper, I'd had to place restrictions on the level of commitment I could give them. When push came to shove, I was a wife and a mother with three kids at home. It wasn't possible to put my domestic life second in a way most of the men could, jumping on a plane and disappearing for weeks on end. That's not to say the men didn't find it stressful to be separated from their families. Kent Gavin once estimated that he'd spent almost six months abroad in a single year. Tough on relationships. But we'd all chosen these high-flying, high-pressure jobs. Six nights a week, those bloody great printing presses had to roll. It was as simple as that.

So in my case it was only in an emergency, when a huge story was breaking and the newsroom was throbbing, that I might be forced to put being a photographer before being a mother. And even then I was never very happy about it. But there were times, in the wee small hours, when I lay awake wondering how much more I might have achieved in my work if my hands hadn't been a bit tied, however willingly I had tied them myself. How many other women are still asking themselves the same question in the far more enlightened 21st century? But in waking hours I pushed those thoughts to a far corner of my mind and got on with the job.

Above all, I was really glad to be working among such a top-class group of professionals. On a rare 'quiet' day, we'd sit around sharing tricks of the trade, chat about technical stuff, how one of us had managed to get an especially great shot or how some crafty sod on another paper had got a better one than any of us.

There is more than one kind of family. And these men, my 'boys', were a second family to me. As in all families, there was the odd little tiff, the occasional feathers ruffled, but never very seriously and never for very long. For twenty-six years, with the inevitable changes of face, they gave me respect, affection, lots of fun and sometimes, when I really needed it, the most amazing support. For all of us, that huge brutal building on Holborn Circus was a second home. For me in particular, it became an escape and a refuge when things in my real home were intolerable.

Chapter Eight

Snapping the Sixties

'How're you feeling, love?' I asked the sad little girl tucked up in her bed.

'Pretty bloody awful, Doreen.'

'Sure you don't mind me doing a few shots? It feels like a right cheek.'

'Not since it's you, Doreen. Not sure I can manage a smile though.'

Lesley Hornby's eyes, big as saucers in her thin little face, looked up at me from just above the covers. She looked like a wounded doe in a forest clearing. Like Christine and Mandy, though in a very different way, she was an ordinary girl who'd become one of the most iconic faces of the age and had to learn how to cope with it. These days they called her Twiggy.

Instead of being in her little bedroom in her parents' house in Neasden, she should have been at the Women of the Year luncheon at the Savoy Hotel. But she'd caught the flu, a mundane event for most people, but not for her. If Twiggy even burped, Britain wanted to know. So the press, including me, had descended on Neasden to get the 'story'. Daft or what?

But I had some credit with Twiggy and her mum, Nellie Hornby. I'd been to the house once before. As I'd arrived, Twiggy had been in a panic because her dog had got out of the garden.

She'd jumped into my car and we'd scoured the streets till we found it. We were chums after that. So if Nellie was going to let anybody in to photograph poor little Lesley, it was going to be me. My mates from the other papers were well cheesed-off.

The shots I got were wonderful, smiles or not. They were real 'pictures'. They showed the superstar model for what she really was. Just a seventeen-year-old who, when she felt rotten, wanted her own bed, her old teddy bear and her mum to look after her. A posh lunch at The Savoy couldn't really compete with that.

Twiggy was, and is, one of the nicest people you could ever hope to meet. The word 'unspoiled' is a cliché, but it was totally true in her case. She was in a tough business but it never changed her. She had no airs and graces and a simple goodness which, by some alchemy, the camera could pick up. Photographing her was always a joy. You just couldn't take a bad picture.

Twiggy's 'look' had become one of the most memorable images of a memorable decade. Those big eyes, the full, almost pouting mouth. She was only five-feet six-inches, small for a model, and weighed about seven stone. Once Leonard, the famous Mayfair hairdresser, had cut her hair short, the flat-chested Twiggy could have passed for a teenage boy. But that androgynous look was part of the spirit of the times. The new fashions of the Sixties suited her perfectly. Her photograph would appear on magazine covers all over the world. During her career, she'd be photographed by all the really big names: Richard Avedon, Norman Parkinson, Annie Leibovitz, Cecil Beaton. Astonishingly, none of it ever turned her head.

My return to the *Daily Mirror* in 1962 couldn't have been better timed. I've already said how London somehow felt different on that first morning. A lighter, brighter town. Something exciting in the air. Even the growing political tensions of the Cold War, the Cuban Missile Crisis and the shocking assassination of President Kennedy couldn't stop a great wind of change sweeping through the culture of the times, especially in Britain, which would give birth to so many aspects of it.

The decade that became known as the Swinging Sixties had several elements. Politics, pop music, drama and film were all in the mix. But it was arguably fashion that drove the whole shebang.

There's a scene in the film *Billy Liar* in which Julie Christie is walking briskly along the pavement of some northern town. Like Twiggy a couple of years later, she is about to become one of the icons of the age. She is young and beautiful. Her long blonde hair moving gently in the breeze. A bag swings from her shoulder. She wears a little make-up but not much. After the over-painted goddesses of Hollywood, there's a freshness about her, as if she's a brand new type of woman. There's an innocence too, a kind of wholesomeness even, which is odd since she's wearing a new fashion that many people regarded as scandalous and even downright immoral. Yes, it's the miniskirt, perhaps the most epoch-making garment ever created. Beneath it, Julie Christie's long slim legs stride out along the street. Heads turn, male and female. This was revolution, pure and simple. The cobwebs were being blown off Britain.

Until now, most British girls still didn't dress all that differently from their own mothers. In 1960, twinsets and pearls were still a common sight on many young women. Some wore their hair in the American ponytail, but plenty still sported the 'Alice' band that had been around since the original Alice had gone down the rabbit-hole.

Till this point, with the exception of Coco Chanel, nearly all the great fashion designers had been men. Dior, Givenchy, Balenciaga. Those snooty Paris couturiers who, like gods on Mount Olympus, sent out decrees on what women must be wearing that year. Women who could afford to followed like sheep. Women who couldn't just went on looking like their mums. It was all pretty boring. Then came the explosion.

The women on the streets, the ones who couldn't afford the likes of Dior, began to create their own fashion, which grew up out of the needs of ordinary lives and was affordable for almost everyone. It was disposable even and could be discarded next year when something else new and exciting came along. It was all a far cry from that 'Sunday best' posh frock that spent most of its life packed away in chiffon and was expected to last you for years. Goodbye to all that.

This fashion revolution was created and nurtured by a relatively small number of talented people. Designers, models, hairdressers, photographers. But the whole thing was powered by the enthusiasm and support of a band of young female journalists in the British press. Without them it wouldn't have taken root in the way that it so triumphantly did. Luckily for me, one of these women was the Fashion Editor of the *Daily Mirror*. A stroke of good fortune that would put me right at the heart of these incredibly buzzy years.

Felicity Green was the right woman in the right place at the right time. She didn't have huge interest in those elegant catwalks of the Rue Saint-Honoré or of their British counterparts, the stately Normal Hartnell or Hardy Amies. She was far more excited by what was parading along Oxford Street. Instead of the ice-cold mannequins with frozen expressions, she liked the perky, chirpy style of the girls who'd popped out to buy a sandwich to take back to their typewriters.

Felicity was inspired by the new breed of clothes designers who reflected that liberation. Young designers who broke all the rules, who didn't work out of grand premises in Mayfair, but from basements in Soho or attics in Chelsea. She put their work in the pages of the *Daily Mirror* where millions of women saw it and adopted it as their own. Some of the stuffy, middle-aged white men on the paper's board were baffled, even disgusted; the chairman Cecil King threatened to fire her. Others like Hugh Cudlipp, though baffled too, had the foresight to realise that something big was afoot and let Felicity have her head. It's a cliché, but Felicity's balls were as big as theirs.

In the Swinging Sixties, the long-running 'Felicity Green on the Fashion Scene' became a bible for every young woman remotely interested in how they looked. It was great working with her. Only five feet tall, always incredibly stylish, she was a little barrel of energy. Indefatigable. Totally committed.

She championed the early design efforts of Barbara Hulanicki, the creator of Biba, one of the most influential fashion brands of its generation. Specifically for the *Mirror*, Hulanicki designed a simple A-line dress in pink gingham with a matching headscarf, offered to readers by mail order for the princely sum of twenty-five shillings. They expected to shift a couple of thousand but instead sold more than 30,000. There was no gingham left in the entire country. And the Biba empire took off. The ultimate Biba store on Kensington High Street was unlike any shop before or since, all feather boas, potted palms and antique hat-stands. Not to mention communal changing-rooms where the supposedly reserved British cheerfully showed their tits and bums to anyone who happened to be there. It really was the coolest shop on earth.

The work of the great Mary Quant was also showcased in Felicity's pages. After the dreary Fifties, Quant was like a burst of sunshine. She was a true phenomenon, not just a fashion designer but the genius behind an entirely fresh look that embraced hair, make-up, underwear, the whole caboodle. It's still argued about exactly who created the miniskirt, but Mary has the best claim, though she says that she only kept on shortening skirts because the customers at her ultra-trendy King's Road shop Bazaar demanded it. From the mini, Quant went on to experiment with the midi, the maxi and hot-pants. There was nothing she wouldn't try. I photographed her several times. She was a class act, very cool and reserved. I was quite surprised when she told Felicity in an interview that her husband had shaved her pubic hair into a heart shape. Felicity printed it. The prudes reported both Felicity and the newspaper to the Press Council, but they got off. Times had definitely changed. God knows how may heart-shaped pubes were walking along the streets of Britain!

For any photographer, this cultural earthquake was a great chance to make your mark. Since the new clothes were all about being young, unstuffy and very different from mummy's generation, the photographs had to be that way too.

As Felicity did, I wanted the models to look like they were enjoying themselves. Isn't the whole point of fashion that it's supposed to be fun? As it had been in the Fifties, the cool image in 2016 is for models to look as if they're standing in front of a firing squad. Back then, I'd have my girls moving about, dancing, laughing, interacting with each other. It shouldn't look like 'modelling', it should look like being alive. Instead of always shooting in a bland studio, we'd go out onto the streets, even to bizarre locations like factories, swimming baths, working men's caffs. Anything went, as long as it was impactful.

Technically, because the pictures were almost always in black and white, you had to make sure the images had strong simple lines so that they leapt off the page. Shooting in colour, you could always hide behind its vibrancy, but there was no hiding place with black and white. Clarity was so important, even in a moody shot. And you always had to remember that newsprint could look a bit grubby if you weren't careful. There was a lot to get right.

The overwhelming thing was to make it look and feel 'real'. So we experimented with using non-professional models. For a long-running series called 'Gorgeous Girls', I used to hang around outside Fenwick, the department store in Bond Street. It was a chic corner of town and lots of the girls who worked around there, in the boutiques, the art galleries, the auction houses, were very fashion-conscious.

'Excuse me, dear, would you mind if I took your photograph?'

'Me? Why? Who are you?'

'I'm from the *Daily Mirror*. I think you look just great. Would you mind your photo going in the paper?'

'In the paper? Oh crikey. Well, I don't know. Gosh, I can't think what to say…'

Of course, when I turned the lens on them, some were as wooden as Fenwick's window frames. They'd really struggle to be natural and I'd have to find ways to disguise that, like sticking them in a phone box or borrowing a passer-by's Pekingese doggie. But enough of them were as relaxed and cool as their clothes and it often worked a treat. It saved the *Mirror* modelling fees too, which always pleased the accountants at Holborn Circus.

The professional models were very different. You couldn't take a 'bad' picture of a Twiggy or a Vicki Hodge. You just stuck them in front of a white backdrop in the studio and more or less left them to it. These girls had studied themselves in the mirror and worked out all their best angles. The Sixties breed of girl was a lot different from their predecessors. Models from the Fifties like Barbara Goalen, Suzy Parker and Bettina had presented themselves to the camera almost as aristocrats who really didn't need to be modelling at all. But these new girls weren't cold or condescending. They were just up for a good time.

Vicki Hodge, with whom I loved to work, was one of those. Vicki, beautiful and slim as a rake, had a voracious appetite.

'I'll do anything you want, Doreen,' she'd say when I rang her up. 'But I'm always starving, so if I need to eat, you'll have to stop.'

Bacon sandwiches, pork pies, chocolate biscuits – everything went down her lovely neck and never seemed to leave a mark on her body. It was the only thing I hated about this great girl.

Once I took Vicki out on the street in a long maxi-coat, accompanied by a Borzoi dog we'd hired for the day. We'd given the dog a matching maxi-coat made out of a blanket. The bloody dog pulled poor Vicki this way and that, almost dragging her off her feet, but the pictures were wonderfully vibrant. Vicki got a bacon sandwich and the dog an extra biscuit.

Another day, she was in a calf-length coat whose gimmick was an adjustable hem. By ripping it off, the coat could be instantly made shorter. We decided to get a passer-by to do this, a real City gent in pinstripes and a bowler hat. The image of this pillar of society revealing a young girl's gorgeous legs made a great photograph. Fun, a bit naughty, catching the spirit of the age. That's what it was all about.

One of the nicest models I shot was an absolute stunner from British Guyana called Shakira Baksh. She came into the *Mirror* studio on what was known in the trade as a 'go-see', when a photographer takes some pictures of a model to decide whether or not they're photogenic. My friend Jean Dobson, who was Felicity Green's assistant and the daughter of a doctor, had a very clinical eye. She always said that 'the grain of the flesh' was the thing that mattered. Shakira Baksh certainly had that, as well as a sweet personality. She'd do anything she could to please you. One day she told me about some chap she'd just met and thought she rather liked.

'I think he's quite well-known,' she said vaguely.

'What's his name dear?' I asked.

'Um… Michael Caine.'

'Bloody hell, you mean you've never heard of Michael Caine?'

A couple of years later, they were married (and still are). The lovely Shakira no longer needed Doreen Spooner or the *Daily Mirror.*

A key element of the Sixties scene was the emergence of the male fashion photographer as a celebrity. David Bailey, Terry O'Neill, Brian Duffy, Terence Donovan. They became the coolest guys in town, driving along the King's Road in open-topped sports cars with what was then called a 'dolly bird'. They mixed with royalty, pop groups and movie stars. They even married movie stars – Bailey got hitched to Catherine Deneuve and Terry O'Neill later wed Faye Dunaway. Their mates were the other Sixties boy-wonders like the afore-mentioned Michael Caine and Terence Stamp.

Several of them were working-class lads from very poor backgrounds, a fact that made them even more alluring as the

Sixties slowly torpedoed many of the previous barriers such as class, gender and, to an extent, race. Part of the reason for the rise of these celebrity snappers was that they themselves had often discovered the iconic models of the times. David Bailey had found the stunning Jean Shrimpton, who was, alongside Twiggy, the most famous model in Britain. And it was a photographer, Barry Lategan, who'd taken the first pictures of Twiggy herself and set her on the road to international fame. It soon got to a point that whoever had taken a photograph was sometimes as much of a draw as the image itself.

And that created a problem. Working with these guys was very much part of the appeal of Felicity Green's hugely influential fashion pages. Not surprisingly, it made the staff photographers on the paper feel slightly like second-class citizens, as if we weren't quite good enough. Though, as I've said, there was rarely professional jealousy among ourselves, it certainly kicked in with regard to the celebrity snappers. When these guys delivered their work to Simon Clyne, the Picture Editor, they presented huge glossy prints. But the staff photographers weren't allowed to do that. To save money we were permitted no bigger than eight-by-six. It didn't seem like a level playing field and that got up our noses. Revolution was rumbling in the photographers' room, but none of the 'boys' had the guts to take the lift to Felicity's office and complain. So I went up and gave it to her, woman to woman. After that, the in-house team were allowed more fashion shoots, though it might have been more because the bosses began to baulk at the high fees demanded by those starry outsiders. We really weren't *Vogue* after all.

That niggle apart, I loved the jobs I did for the fashion pages. Felicity was always stimulating and great fun. We had an interesting time in 1967 when we went to Moscow as part of a British Board of Trade Delegation to promote British fashion. It was a bit like Britain right after the war – a grey, depressed place where the shops had almost nothing in them and people had to queue for everything, including bread. The Russian women were a sadly drab lot, starved of frivolities of any kind. When we took the models out of the exhibition halls and onto the streets, the women looked unimpressed rather than excited. They must have thought we were completely spoilt and decadent. Maybe we were. Once we came across a long queue of women and eventually found out what they were waiting for so patiently. The answer was bras. Great big bras too, real boulder-holders. There certainly weren't many Twiggys in Moscow. Maybe it was all those potatoes. The *Daily Mirror* may have been a left-wing paper but, after my first glimpse of the USSR, I'd certainly never be going to work for the *Morning Star*.

In the Sixties, the worlds of fashion, pop and acting were closely intertwined, feeding off each other, the boundaries blurred. Pop groups, solo singers and performers needed to be seen in the latest gear, so I had to shoot an endless parade of the glitterati. The fifteen-year-old Scottish dynamo Lulu, performing her first big hit *Shout*, never lost patience no matter how many times she was asked to cup her hands around her mouth. Sandie Shaw, with her trademark bare feet, in the dress in which she'd won Eurovision singing *Puppet on a String*. The ethereal Marianne Faithfull, looking like a typical English rose but who, being Mick Jagger's girlfriend, was nothing of the sort. The spunky, no-nonsense Cilla Black, arm in arm with Tommy Nutter, the hippest tailor of the day. And Diana Rigg who, as Emma Peel in *The Avengers* modelled the stunning fashions of the designer John Bates.

I shot many of the cool Sixties boys too. The young Sean Connery, the definitive James Bond, an instant worldwide star after *Dr No*. Dudley Moore and Peter Cook, the new Young Turks of anti-Establishment comedy. The great musician Leonard Bernstein conducting at the Festival Hall.

But the Sixties couldn't last, of course, either literally or spiritually. Every revolution eventually runs out of steam. By the end of the decade, things were a good bit darker. The Vietnam

War, the student protests of '68, the Russian invasion of Czechoslovakia, the Sharon Tate murders. Even The Beatles split up in 1970. Hippy culture had arrived and everything got a bit more flowery and druggy. Those sharp black and white lines of the early Sixties were gradually softened, became more prettified, more insubstantial.

But though everything had to move on, the creative surge that had happened, especially in London, had shaken up British society once and for all. Those cobwebs had well and truly blown away. As the British Empire gradually blew away too, we'd found an unexpected new role for ourselves as a hotbed of innovation and creativity which, arguably, gave us just as much economic clout in the wider world. What a time it was. And I was so bloody lucky to have been a part of it.

These years were the golden age of the *Daily Mirror*. At its peak it sold well over five-million copies a day, which meant a probable readership of around fifteen-million people, roughly one in three of the British population. A world-record for any newspaper. The *Mirror* seemed as much part of the landscape as the White Cliffs of Dover, fish and chips and the Union Jack. Vast numbers were addicted to its cartoon characters Andy Capp, Garth and The Perishers, all of which ran for decades. In the summer months, thousands wandered the seaside proms trying to spot a man called 'Chalky White', whose fuzzy image had been shown in the paper. If you thought you'd identified him, you had to accost him and say, 'To my delight it's Chalky White and I claim my £5.'

To celebrate its spectacular success, a huge party was held in the Royal Albert Hall. There was a really good cabaret that night. The Beatles. That's how prestigious the *Daily Mirror*, the paper started in 1903 for genteel Edwardian ladies, had become.

Women like Felicity Green and Marje Proops had played a huge role in that success. In their different ways, they'd forced the big cheeses on the top floor to realise that the country was moving on fast and that they'd be wise to keep up. Suddenly the things that women cared about could no longer be shunted off into pages near the back. Suddenly these issues were front-page news, right at the heart of what the country was getting excited about, from the clothes they wanted to wear to the roles they wanted to play in a different, more equal Britain. Those stuffy, macho Fleet Street attitudes would have to change. If they didn't, the *Mirror* might wave bye-bye to a big chunk of its readership. Luckily, those 'old buffers' took the hint and allowed the paper to undergo a personality change. No longer just the working man's paper, lampooned in its most famous cartoon character 'Andy Capp', but a more enlightened newspaper altogether. Still instantly accessible and easy to read, but a bit more thoughtful, a bit more adventurous and a hell of a lot more fun.

I like to think that I played a small role in that change of character. Not just because of my photographs, but just by being there. Never waving any big feminist flag or coming into work without my bra (though Felicity did, at least once). Just by turning up every morning and getting on with the job. Doing whatever assignment was given to me. Never using my gender as an excuse. And never ever being a diva (something Felicity and Marje, much as I loved them both, could sometimes be).

But there was one fashion job everybody loathed. Royal Ascot. What a pain in the arse that was. Every year it was the same. A bloody great scrum. If the paper had managed to get you a pass for the Royal Enclosure, at least you'd be jostled and crushed by people who'd been to a good school. If it hadn't, it was a nightmare. Not remotely like the Ascot scene in *My Fair Lady*. More like the Brighton Pier on a Bank Holiday, but with big hats. And so many of those hats were just plain silly. The office would tell you that some famous so-and-so was going to be there and you'd better get back with a great shot. But half the time the celebrity would be wearing a hat so vast it was nearly impossible to capture their face, which kind of defeated the object.

The best shot I ever got at Ascot wasn't of some dolly bird in daft headgear. It was of two blokes. Two very famous blokes – the cricketers Freddie Truman and Ted Dexter. Trussed up in their top hats and tails, they looked so wonderfully out of place that it made a bizarre and wonderful 'picture'. In my mind, the blunt Yorkshireman Truman was saying, 'What a load of old bollocks this is.' But no doubt we ran a more polite caption.

'Right, boys,' I said one year in the photographers' room as the dreaded time approached. 'I've decided to take my holiday during Ascot week.'

There was a collective gasp. Jaws dropped. Coffee cups froze in mid-air.

'Oh, Doreen, please no!' somebody begged.

'You'd surely not do that to us, would you, love?'

I wasn't too keen on Wimbledon either, but the fashion revolution of the Sixties had stretched its tentacles into sport as well and the dresses of the women players often grabbed a headline. This was largely due to the work of a designer called Teddy Tinling. Before Teddy, most female tennis players wore outfits that made them look like their great-aunts. Tinling changed all that. His tennis dresses could have been worn to walk down Carnaby Street or the King's Road, Chelsea. They were different, dazzling and occasionally slightly indecent. The stuffy old tennis establishment was quite shocked. Tinling dresses were worn by a roll-call of women champions including Virginia Wade, Billie Jean King and Martina Navratilova.

Thankfully, Teddy often held photo-calls for his latest collection, usually at the spectacular roof-garden of Derry & Toms in Kensington High Street. The press was grateful for this as it saved us the tedious trek out to suburban SW19. One year I was late and arrived to find Teddy drumming his fingers on a table and a crowd of irritated press people. He'd refused to start the show till I got there.

'Perhaps we can begin now. Mrs *Daily Mirror* has arrived.'

Amazing, the power of fifteen-million readers.

Chapter Nine

Heartbreak

Dear Marje didn't approve of divorce. Despite her progressive position on almost everything else, she thought it was an admission of defeat, especially when children were involved. That was presumably why she stayed married to the long-suffering 'Proopsie', decades after she'd deserted his bed and jumped into someone else's. It was fine to go into an Ann Summers shop in search of sexy underwear, but not into a divorce court. As time went on, she softened her views a bit, but they were firmly held in the mid-1960s.

Most of the country would have agreed with her. I certainly did. It was nearly thirty years since Edward VIII had married the twice-divorced Mrs Simpson, almost ten since the divorced Group Captain Townsend had been declared an unthinkable husband for Princess Margaret, but it still carried a surprising social stigma. Even the starry example of Elizabeth Taylor, the gorgeous girl with the violet eyes who'd already dumped three husbands, couldn't quite change that, even if we all lapped up the lurid details in the press. For most ordinary people, the break-up of a marriage, especially if it had been consecrated in a church, remained a slightly shocking thing. Even the 'innocent' party would be tainted by it, carrying it around with them like a faintly bad smell.

In 1962, when the crisis hit my marriage, I didn't want us to split up. We had a home and I wanted to keep it together. I still loved the man whose proposal I'd accepted ten years before on the Pont Saint-Louis. We'd known great happiness together, our photo albums were jam-packed with wonderful memories. Besides, I didn't want to bring up three young kids on my own. How in God's name would I do that?

That's not to say the subject of divorce wasn't raised. My Dad, who'd helped us financially to weather the immediate storm, had suggested it. He and I were still very close and it pained him to see his little girl in such dire straits. Naturally, he was angry and disgusted with Pierre, even though I'd played down the worst of it, making excuses as much as possible. He never admitted it, but I suspect Dad might have lent him money in the past. If so, it had gone straight across the bar counters of Fleet Street.

Besides, the notion that I was partly to blame had already wormed its way inside me, where it would remain till Pierre's death. It's still there today. The worst thing, surely, would be to walk away from this man who'd got himself into such a terrible mess. The fact that he'd got me and the kids into the mess too was lousy, but we were a family after all. Wasn't that what I'd always wanted? Wasn't that what Pierre had given me? Whatever trouble he'd caused, what sort of wife would turn her back on him now? It would be a shameful, disgraceful thing to do. We'd go forward, we'd struggle on, somehow we'd get over this.

And, within limitations, for long periods of time, we did. I'd gone back to work, money was coming in again, the house was safe. As far as I could tell, the kids were all young enough to be largely unaware of what had happened, though it's hard to believe they hadn't sensed some change in the atmosphere.

But though the immediate crisis had been averted, the causes of it were still there. I was bright enough to realise that. If those weren't resolved, mightn't the crisis raise its head again? What more could I do to make my husband happy?

Go back to France? But the two older kids were firmly settled in

NO BUSINESS LIKE... Ugly Sisters Sir Robert Helpmann and Sir Frederick Ashton (above) look glum as the Royal Ballet's Cinderella (Margot Fonteyn) finds her Prince (David Blair), 1965. Sophia Loren (below left) was "p***ed off", but more beautiful for it. Chirpy Russell Harty (below right) adopts a 'grim up North' pose

SWINGING SIXTIES Even when unwell, 17-year-old Twiggy (above) was a gift to the camera. Copying her trademark spiky eyelashes led to excess: the longest false eyelashes in the world (below left), from 1968. The mini and the Mini – a photographic match made in heaven (below right)

WOMEN ON THE RISE Sandie Shaw (above left), shoeless in pink chiffon, dressed just as she appeared the next day for her 1967 Eurovision win. Marianne Faithfull (above right) in her first, waiflike, incarnation aged 18. In the same year, 1964, Diana Rigg (below) made a tougher character as The Avengers' action woman Emma Peel

MOVIE MAGIC Effortlessly elegant French actress Capucine (above), star of The Pink Panther, shot before the 1964 premiere. From radio to TV to Hollywood, Marty Feldman (below left), "an amazing face to photograph". Actress Charlotte Rampling (below right), with soon-to-be husband composer Jean-Michel Jarre in 1977

STYLE ICONS Part-punk, part-Monroe, Debbie Harry (above left) and her band Blondie provided the soundtrack for the 1980s. Bestselling novelist Harold Robbins (above right on his yacht in St Tropez in 1980) left Doreen cold. Fashion guru Yves St Laurent opened his Rive Gauche store in New Bond Street in 1969

THAT BIT EXTRA Context can make a picture: Doreen found a maxi-coat for the dog to match model Vicki Hodge's (above) and she photographed composer Leonard Bernstein amid abandoned instruments in a rehearsal break at the Fairfield Halls, Croydon

STAR PERFORMERS American playwright Tennessee Williams gives his all at a 1962 London press conference (above). Even from her bed, 75-year-old poet Edith Sitwell (below left) is a commanding presence. Young Russian Olympic gymnast Olga Korbut (below right, meeting PM Edward Heath) charmed the world in the 1970s

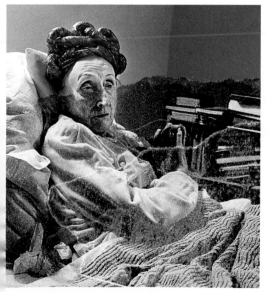

MUSIC, MUSIC, MUSIC Doreen thought it would be fun to shoot jazz violinist Stéphane Grappelli (above) in busker mode in 1970 and it "worked a treat". But it was glamour all the way with Spandau Ballet (below) when they were recording their album, True, in the Bahamas in 1982

their schools. They'd been dragged to and fro enough, especially Tony, who was nearly ten now. In Paris, Pierre's much-loved stepfather Raymond Manevy had died suddenly, soon after we'd moved to London, a loss that hit Pierre hard and must have contributed to his sense of being cut off from the life he'd once known. His mother, Mègaby, now trying to cope with widowhood, obviously had her own troubles, some of which were financial. Besides, she was far from the most maternal of women. Pierre wouldn't get many cuddles there. By an odd chance, Pierre's half-brother Alain, the journalist, had moved to London and was working in the *Daily Mirror* building. Maybe that might help Pierre settle, I thought. If his brother could adapt to life in England, why shouldn't he? It was difficult to see what would be gained by traipsing back to Paris.

But what about the drinking? What was to be done about that? I've already said that I'd noticed his consumption had gone up sharply, but had turned a blind, careless eye. That French thing. Just joie de vivre, nothing more. But now it was clearly a great deal more. I'd heard of Alcoholics Anonymous. It had been going in the UK for over twenty years. But surely that was for the down and outs on the Embankment, not for a 'gentleman' like Pierre? And wasn't the AA partly about letting Jesus into your life? Giving yourself over to the Lord? Sitting in a circle of chairs, telling total strangers that you were an alcoholic? Pierre would never have admitted it for a start, certainly not to himself. And perhaps I didn't either. In those days, the idea that drinking too much was an actual illness, something outside the sufferer's control, was still quite new, at least to the man or woman in the street. To most folk, it was just a defect of character. You sorted it out by getting a grip of yourself, turning over a new leaf, that sort of thing. Pull your socks up, mate.

So, how could I make my husband into a happier man? I couldn't think of anything except love. Love and support. The stability of a wife and children who adored him. And for the next fifteen years, through some truly awful times, that was what I tried to do.

But Pierre needed a cuddle not just from his loved ones in Shortlands, but from those in Fleet Street. I found it hard to understand why they wouldn't embrace his talent in the way it deserved. The xenophobia thing might explain it to some extent. The only other contributory cause was that, as I've said before, my husband perhaps wasn't a 'man's man'. He loved the company of women. He'd always been an enthusiastic, outgoing host, the proprietor of 'Pierre's Bistro' back in the house at Bois-Colombes. He was great fun at a dinner party – intelligent, warm, amusing. But maybe he wasn't quite what the British call 'clubbable'. He'd not really want to spend three hours in a pub discussing the cricket scores, the fortunes of Arsenal or the best vegetables to plant in a north-facing allotment. He was too bright to do that for long. Pierre came from that grand apartment in the Rue de la Planche, the stepson of one of France's most respected intellects. He'd studied at L'École Des Beaux-Arts, where Delacroix, Renoir and Seurat had studied before him.

The world of British tabloid journalism was a long way from all that. While the 'serious' broadsheet papers were often staffed by Oxbridge graduates, the mass market papers were frequently inhabited by those who'd left school early and started their careers as tea-boys, 'runners' or typists. That's not to say for one second they weren't brilliantly talented newspaper people, just that the culture was different.

But it seemed only too obvious that Pierre had tried to mix in. Tried way too hard in fact. Dutifully, he'd gone to the pub after work, bought his rounds, pretended to get interested in the doings of Geoff Boycott or Bobby Charlton. But maybe, as he realised that he was never going to be 'one of the boys', he'd had another drink to ease the loneliness of that. At the time of the crisis, I found out that he owed money in several Fleet Street watering holes.

There were periods though when everything seemed not too bad. Pierre still got some decent work. He still loved showbiz, especially musicians. He managed to get access to the Fab Four at the very height of Beatlemania. The shots, mostly taken backstage in bleak theatre dressing rooms, are brilliant. After a while, John, Paul, George and Ringo seem to have forgotten he was there, which is every photographer's objective. They dropped the jaunty grins, the larking about. They were tired and it showed. The pictures of John Lennon, looking so young, are especially touching in the knowledge of what would happen to him. To me, they're even more touching in the light of what would happen to Pierre. The two of them would die in the same year, long before their time.

By now, Pierre had left the *Daily Sketch* and gone to the *Daily Express*, but only as a freelancer. Unfortunately, being a freelancer only marginalised him even more. He was no more 'one of the boys' there that he'd been at the *Sketch*. Even at the *Mirror*, we'd never really consider freelance photographers as one of the gang. Shitty really. Freelancers were mostly called in when the permanent photographers were overstretched. Their working hours were sometimes awful. The jobs they were given were often of less interest, the bread-and-butter stuff, frequently tedious. And the poorer the quality of your recent work, the less likely you were to be given a great opportunity to prove yourself. It was catch-22.

From that morning when my scoop with Christine and Mandy had landed on our kitchen table, I had seen his envy of my working life grow. He tried to hide it but I knew it was there. When I got home in the evenings, I began to talk less about what I'd been doing that day, especially if it was glamorous or exciting. I missed doing that, not because I wanted to brag but because I wanted to share my day with the person most important to me. But sometimes, the *Mirror* would land again on the kitchen table, open at a page of my latest pictures.

'You never said you were shooting Frank Sinatra,' he'd say.

'Oh, I forgot, love. Only took half an hour.'

I soon realised the necessity of underplaying my own achievements in order not to rub his nose in his own situation.

But somehow, the household in Valley Road kept itself together. We'd had a long string of German au pairs to look after the kids when Pierre and I were at work. Rosemary, who'd been in Bois-Colombes, came with us to London for a while. When she left, she found us a replacement from her own village and this strange but pleasant process went on for the next decade. Gudrun, Barbara and others whose names I've shamefully forgotten.

These girls must have sensed the tensions in the air sometimes, but the presence of a 'stranger' in the house forced us to keep a lid on them as much as possible. Having a young cheery girl around was also good for the kids and often for me too. It was always a wrench when it was time for one of them to go home to their own country.

'My darling, you can always fly over and see me,' said one, trying to comfort a tearful little Catherine.

'But I can't fly!' she wailed. 'I don't have any wings!'

After the trauma of the bailiff, I've no doubt that Pierre made a major effort to control his drinking. An effort that would continue right up till the day he died. The 'battle with the bottle' might be a cliché but it's tragically true. These days, there's so much more help available to anyone fighting it. Then it was a very different matter.

If Pierre's battle chalked up quite a few victories, those days when he managed not to drink, there were just as many defeats. I could tell which sort of day it was the moment he put his key in the door and I looked at his face. In time, as they got older, the children would develop the same skill.

'Dad's in a funny mood again,' was the expression we usually used.

Jeanne now says she began to wonder if all fathers acted in the same way. She even went round quizzing her school friends about how theirs behaved.

It was an awful thing to see a different person emerge from inside the man I'd fallen in love with. When he was sober, Pierre Vandeputte was a wonderful husband and devoted dad. When he was drunk, there was a stranger under our roof. Somebody we didn't much like, were even afraid of at times, but who we still deeply loved.

The booze eventually began to take its toll on his health, of course. The constant Gauloises didn't help either, but half the world smoked back then. He was forty by now, nudging middle age and, considering how he mistreated his body, that began to show. The lovely jet-black hair had thinned out, the face became puffy. I began to miss my handsome Frenchman.

The drink affected more than his physical health. Always a highly emotional man, the alcohol could multiply that characteristic many times over. In 1966, one of the worst tragedies in British history occurred in the small Welsh village of Aberfan, when a huge tip of coal slurry slid down a mountain and killed 144 people, nearly all of them children. The world's press descended and Pierre was among them. It was chaos. Frantic rescue efforts were made but one by one the bodies of the children were excavated from the filthy mud. Even the toughest press and TV people were devastated by the things they saw and Pierre, by this stage, was far from tough. He was a family man himself. He adored Tony, Jeanne and Catherine and seeing the grief of the parents at Aberfan was too much for him.

He wasn't the only press person to reach for a drink that day, but he probably swallowed more than most. He'd rushed to Wales by car and, on the way back, he slammed it into the back of a lorry. His injuries were minor, but he lost his sense of smell. His licence was taken away for a while, but they were less draconian then and it was eventually returned to him. It wouldn't be the last time he lost it.

Though I tried to minimise it, there were occasions at the *Mirror* when I was forced to make a trip away. Sometimes just for a night, but sometimes for several days, as when I went with Felicity Green to Moscow or to fashion shows in Paris or Rome.

When I had to go away, I'd always find it hard to make that walk down the path and turn towards the station. If I looked back, little Catherine would often be standing at the front window, looking bereft and waving me off. When I got back, Pierre too would always be a little moist-eyed and say how much he'd missed me. It's just as well I didn't know till many years later that, after I'd gone, he would usually break down and weep. If the au pair was out at her language classes, he'd cook something for the children then hit the bottle on his own.

He was still working freelance, doing the best he could to bring in some money, but by now I was earning far more than he was. Even today, that sort of disparity can cause tensions in a relationship. In those days, it could be a really hard thing for a man to handle. Further back, when I'd first worked for the *Mirror* in the late Forties, a boy I really fancied broke things off because he couldn't cope with the fact that his Army salary was lower than mine. For most men, it seemed to be like having their balls chopped off.

Poor Pierre. He must have been unhappy on so many fronts. His wife keeping the roof over their heads. Not getting the work his talent deserved. Fighting a daily battle with a terrible addiction. Above all perhaps, remorse at the pain he knew he was causing me.

Every summer, the kids were sent for a month-long holiday with Mègaby in the country. Nothing much had changed under Mègaby's roof. The sorrows of widowhood hadn't mellowed her in the slightest. She still ruled the table like a tyrant. How I missed the warm, sweet presence of Raymond behind his pipe and his arms thrown wide to hug me.

'Ma petite Anglaise!'

She was very hard on the children. A month at Mègaby's wasn't that dissimilar to being at an army camp. There were lots of rules and regulations. She was determined that Jeanne and Catherine should grow up as very proper little ladies. Good manners and etiquette were drummed into them. Once, Jeanne was caught stealing a sweet from her grandmother's bedroom. Mègaby grabbed her and stuffed so many sweets into her mouth that she almost choked. A dangerous punishment. No wonder the kids were a bit scared of her. To this day, Jeanne calls her a 'witch'.

Pierre and I would join them for part of the time. It wasn't much of a holiday for him either. He and his mother still fought as much as they had ever done. I could never quite understand why. The youngest brother, Alain, her only child by Raymond Manevy, was always the apple of her eye. It was usually Jean and, in particular, Pierre who got the worst of it. Possibly the brothers looked like her former husband, constant physical reminders of that disastrous first marriage. Mègaby seemed to require perfection from those around her and few of us could live up to that. Obviously, as Pierre's drinking got a tighter grip on him, he certainly couldn't. He tried to hide it from his mother, but she was nobody's fool. When she decided to make a cherry tart for which the first step was to soak the fruit in alcohol, Pierre drained off the alcohol and replaced it with water, thinking she'd never know. But unlike alcohol, water rotted the cherries, leaving just a soggy mess. What rows took place behind my back, I shudder to think. Appearances were important to Mègaby and must be maintained at all costs. But the bottom line was that Pierre certainly found no solace or support from his mother.

Luckily, we had another escape route from our lives in London. We'd bought a caravan, which was kept at Deal on the Kent coast and we went there whenever we could. It was a big caravan, luxurious even, with separate bedrooms for us and the kids. I hoped fresh air and a change of scene might bring Pierre some sort of peace of mind and reduce his need for the booze.

We all loved it there and, while the kids played on the beach, it gave us some time alone together to talk about the old times. Our little flat in the Latin Quarter. Our walks along the Seine when we were courting. Pushing Tony in the pram through the Jardin du Luxembourg. Memories of the way we were. Despite everything, we still loved each other. There was no doubt about that. But the good old days, unblemished by pain, regret and disappointment, had certainly gone.

And the drinking went on. Pierre was Jekyll and Hyde. In his sober patches, the kids and I adored him as much as we'd always done. At those times, I'd get a short surge of hope that maybe, at long last, his efforts at stopping were finally going to be successful. I knew how hard he tried and I saw his remorse when he failed yet again. But the love that the kids and I gave him clearly wasn't enough. In my ignorance, I still clung to the idea that it was within his power simply to stop. I'd tried to enlist the help of our local GP, who was also a close family friend, being the husband of my old friend Fay from my evacuee years in Wisbech. Would he please talk to Pierre, give him a bollocking, emphasise the damage being done to his health? Sadly, he was next to useless, an 'old school' doctor uncomfortable at dealing with such an issue, especially in somebody he knew. He even went with Pierre to the local pub. Unbelievable.

If only I'd searched around for more serious help. But I didn't. Balancing my hectic job with giving enough time to the children was a hard task. Sometimes, I'd still be up at midnight, sewing the tears in their school uniforms. There was precious little time to deal with Pierre's problem on top of all that. But I should have found it and I didn't. I'll always regret that.

My only other excuse is that I simply didn't know where to look. Marje Proops suggested AA of course, but that was still an impossible option. I'd never have got him there in a hundred years. People said that an alcoholic had to hit rock bottom before he or she would reach out for help. Pierre wasn't there yet. I wondered how I'd cope when he reached it.

Chapter Ten

Life Behind the Lens

I'd have gone mad without the *Mirror*. If Pierre's escape from what ailed him was into alcohol, mine was into my work. It was what got me through the rough times. The companionship. The fun. The knowledge that I was using my talents to the full. All the things my poor husband didn't have.

But it was a high-pressure life. Physically tiring too. That's definitely one reason why female press photographers have been so rare. Camera equipment was heavy, certainly back then, and carrying it around, often in a rush, was back-breaking work. Sometimes almost literally. In the early days, we had to have two cameras, one for the black-and-white pictures used in Britain and another for the colour shots being pioneered in Ireland. You needed not just good health, but real stamina. God knows where mine came from. Nearly every photographer I've known has had physical problems at some point in their career. Poor Arthur Sidey, the animals man, became half-crippled and had to resort to surgery.

Luckily, for all the staff's aches and pains, the *Daily Mirror* employed a permanent masseur. He was a genius – and totally blind. Presumably his disability made his sense of touch more acute. He could instantly track down the most stressed-out, bad-tempered muscle and persuade it to relax and smile again.

'When Jack and Jill went up the hill to fetch a pail of water, how do you think they carried the pails?' he'd always say. 'Across both shoulders. Never on one! You must always distribute the load.'

It was the best advice I ever got. That massage bench was a refuge to which I often crawled in the middle of a busy time. A quiet day was a rarity. We were usually rushing to somewhere or other, laden down with our gear. At least it kept me slim. In my line of work, you could shovel in the chips and it rarely showed on the hips.

If a really big story was breaking, all hell could break loose. Organised, professional, hell, but hell nevertheless. Obviously, the medium of television moved quicker than the press, so we had a TV set in the photographers' room and if we weren't able to get our own shots quickly enough, we'd set up a tripod and just photograph the TV screen. Hardly great quality, but just about possible in extremis.

Out in the main newsroom, the Picture Editor and the News Editor would be yelling across to each other

'What pics have you got on this story now, Len?'

'Not a lot yet, mate. Still coming in.'

'For fuck's sake, I need something like yesterday.'

'Keep your wig on. They're on their way.'

And so it would go. When the pressure was on, the room got noisier, hotter and sweatier. The fag intake, always heavy, shot up even more. The journalists' typewriters hammered away like demented woodpeckers. You needed to keep a fairly cool head.

In any newspaper, the coolest head had to belong to the overall Editor. In my career, I rarely had much to do with these 'grand' Editors, usually just if he wanted his picture taken. In the Sixties, it was Lee Howard, a big beefy bloke who drank like a fish but had a reputation as one of the finest newspaper brains on Fleet Street. It was under his reign that the paper reached its incredible five-million circulation. He was followed by Tony Miles and then by Mike Molloy, who'd begun his career at the *Mirror* as a messenger boy and risen to the very top. That was one of the most admirable aspects of the Fleet Street tabloids – the old-school-tie snobbery that permeated the more 'serious' papers didn't apply. All that mattered was that you had talent; nobody cared which school you'd gone to. We were a Labour paper after all and practised what we preached.

These Editors were the men who had an overview of what the paper should be and where it was going; the guardians of its identity. They were the ones who schmoozed at Number 10 or even in Buckingham Palace. The mass-market press was a powerful means of speaking to the nation and, ever since the early 20th century, those who ran the country had known it. The legendary press barons like Northcliffe and Beaverbrook had always been courted by the great, the good and even by the downright wicked. Though he'd never been elected by anyone, the Editor of the *Daily Mirror* was an important man.

Every night at six, the daily editorial conference took place to finally decide what went into tomorrow's paper and what priority the stories would be given. This was a bit like the conclave of cardinals at the Vatican, led by the Editor himself with the News Editor, the Picture Editor, the Features Editor etc. Minions like photographers were not present.

Obviously the big news stories came first, then features, then sport. There was always the Forward Diary too, a very important document that listed all the up-and-coming events that would need to be covered. A royal tour abroad. A state visit to London. Some big trial. Ascot. Henley. Wimbledon. The Cup Final. As these dates approached, space would need to be earmarked for them and the relevant staff assigned to the job. Every night, it was like putting a huge jigsaw together.

It was possible to get a picture into tomorrow's paper till around nine o'clock in the evening. Then the giant presses in the bowels of the building stretched themselves and began to roll. There was a mad rush of knackered journalists towards the pubs of Fleet Street – though in my case, it was usually straight to the station and back home.

After we'd all crashed into our beds, shattered, pissed or possibly both, delivery vans would be speeding through the dark, deserted streets towards the big railway termini. Stacks of newspapers were thrown onto the trains and taken to every corner of the country, where more vans would rush them to tens of thousands of newsagents in every town and village. There, some sleepy schoolboy on a bike would have got up at dawn in order to shove them through the letter boxes of the nation. This was Fleet Street at its zenith and a bloody impressive operation it was too.

I said before that, in any newspaper office, the enemy was time. There was never enough of it and it was always running out. But, for a staff photographer, there was another threat. The agency photographer. These were the guys from Keystone, Magnum, Black Star or Associated Press who went out to cover stories and then sold the results to the Picture Editors of Fleet Street or to the glossy magazines. That's how my Dad had known the likes of Karl Gullers, Henri Cartier-Bresson and Robert Capa. And of course that's what I'd been myself when I had gone on my tour of America all those years before, and the same when Audrey Whiting had coaxed me over to Paris. Some of the most talented photographers worked for agencies.

But to staff photographers on newspapers, they were the competition. Every big paper had a contract with one agency or another. It was a sort of insurance policy. Almost any story worth getting would be covered by agency people as well as the paper's own permanent team. The agency snappers would then wire their pictures through to the Picture Editor, who'd often have them already spread out on his desk before his own team had scuttled breathlessly out of the *Mirror*'s darkroom. To justify your existence, your pics needed to be better than the agency's. That didn't always happen, and if it didn't happen often enough maybe doubts would arise as to why you were employed.

'Bring me something different!' bleated your Picture Editor, so often that you heard it in your sleep.

So it was a daily challenge to do your best every time. Often in really difficult circumstances. It was one thing doing a nice fashion job in the calm of a studio, just you and the model. But it was another thing altogether to be in the heaving scrum at a big news story or at what was known as a photo-call.

The 'photo-call' was an event where you were squashed in with the photographers from every other newspaper to photograph somebody all at the same time, usually a movie star or a pop singer. It could be a right fight sometimes. It was hard to do your best possible work when you were crammed together like sardines in a tin. But you really had to try.

'Oh, please excuse me, Doreen. I'm so sorry I bumped into you. Do go forward to the front of the group. Gentlemen, please make way for this lady!'

My chances of ever hearing that were exactly zero.

The toughest thing about the photo-call wasn't the physical crush, but the need to be as creative and imaginative as possible within those confines. Your brain needed to be needle-sharp in order to stand a chance of getting something special and beating whatever those agency sods might come up with.

So you'd take a look at Engelbert Humperdinck, Diana Ross, Cliff Richard or whoever was the centre of attention and, while you were clicking away doing conventional shots, try and dream up something just a little bit different. You literally had to think on your feet. If you had an idea, you'd sneak up to the PR person of Engelbert, Diana or Cliff and whisper in their ear.

'Hey, don't you think it'd make a really fab picture if Engelbert, Diana or Cliff stuck their head back between their legs/balanced that champagne bottle on their head/ate that banana/was peeping out from behind that potted palm?'

Often, you'd be told to get lost. But if you were lucky, the PR person would put it to the star and you might get an extra five minutes with them on their own at the end of the photo-call and, hopefully, a great photograph on the front page next day. The star would be pleased, you'd be pleased and, above all, your Picture Editor would be pleased and decide that, after all, it was worth paying your very healthy salary.

To every staff photographer, the Picture Editor was God. I was always lucky with mine: Simon Clyne, Alec Wimburgh, Len Greener. Each with their own little likes and dislikes, some easier than others. Simon, the man who'd taken me back into the paper in 1962, was a benign dictator. He could shout and scream but his heart was in the right place and you knew that he cared about your work almost as much as you did yourself. His successor Alec Wimburgh was very different – a quiet, deeply religious man, a total professional, a safe pair of hands. Then with Len Greener, a great breath of fresh air blew through the photographers' room. A good bit younger than me, full of fresh, exciting ideas, he kept you on your toes. I respected all these men and trusted their judgement. Sometimes it was better than mine.

When you rushed back into the paper from wherever you'd been, you'd go straight to the darkroom and develop your negatives and hang them up to dry. Heaven knows what harm we did to our lungs by breathing those strong chemicals, though most of us lived to tell the tale. Then the darkroom technicians would take your negatives and deliver your 'contacts', printed pages of all your pictures but at thumbnail size. You'd look at these and put a mark on the ones you thought were best. But when the 'contacts' reached the desk of the Picture Editor he'd often disagree with your choice. There might often be heated discussion but, in the end, he was boss. But I'd seen all that when I was a girl, visiting my father at the picture desk of the *Daily Herald*, so I knew the rules of the game.

Felicity Green always maintained that I was a lousy judge of my own work and sometimes overruled not just me but the Picture Editor too. By then she was an even bigger boss than him, the first woman to have a seat on the board of a British newspaper.

Nobody overruled Felicity. Heaven help anyone who tried.

The Picture Editor, aka 'God', even laid down which camera we had to use. In the early days of my career, photographers usually provided their own equipment, but later on, in the big newspapers, such matters were decreed from on high. That could be a really tough experience because your camera often became like an extension of your arms. Being ordered to change to another one could be like losing a limb. The earlier cameras were achingly big and unwieldy, but they gradually became smaller and lighter, which was a godsend to a press photographer dashing around town from one urgent job to another. Many Picture Editors were conservative creatures. It took us ages to persuade Simon Clyne that the new generation of cameras had the same quality as the old monsters. Eventually he embraced the modern age and we were all issued with the latest Pentax, presented to us in a sumptuous leather case. Each was worth around £1,500 even back then. It felt like being handed an MBE.

Despite the physical stresses and the emotional pressure, the sheer unpredictability of the work was something of which I never tired. As I've said, the primary job description of the staff photographer was that you had to do whatever was thrown at you. Mrs Thatcher in the morning, a gorilla at the zoo in the afternoon (no prizes for guessing which was easier).

A major qualification for the job was having what are now called 'people skills'. Back then, we just called it 'getting along'. A big percentage of the work involved interaction with other human beings, even if you never actually spoke to them. If you weren't good at that, you'd never make a successful photographer. I'd realised that right back at the start of my career when I'd photographed King Carl Gustaf of Sweden as a toddler who didn't always do exactly as he was told. You had to weigh up the situation. Evaluate their attitude to being photographed at all. Was the subject addicted to it, as some celebrities were, only really coming alive in front of a lens? Or was it worse than having a root canal? You'd never know till you walked into the room.

Sometimes, the really brave soul would deliberately make the subject cross. The famous portrait photographer Karsh was once shooting Winston Churchill. He was trying to capture that 'bulldog' look, but wasn't quite getting it. On a mad impulse, he snatched the cigar out of Churchill's hand, instantly got the angry snarl he wanted and the picture became famous round the world. A risky business, but the point is that a good photographer can, with subtlety, diplomacy, charm or even downright cheek, get what he or she wants from that person in front of the lens.

With so-called 'ordinary' people, you'd always have to be especially sensitive. Occasionally, you'd come across a 'natural', but often you'd have to work hard to relax them. This was particularly true if the feature was a serious or even tragic one. Snapping girls outside Fenwick in Bond Street was one thing, pointing your camera at a mother whose daughter has been murdered by a maniac is quite another.

A colleague of mine always said that a good press photographer often had to be like a social worker. You had to grasp the ins and outs of people and understand what made them tick. Obviously, the same was true for a journalist doing an interview. If a reporter and a photographer knew how to work together, it could be a very productive double act. Since the very start of my career, I'd realised that my gender could sometimes be a valuable asset. My bosses and my workmates had understood it too. A lot of journalism can be about getting under people's defences and often a woman could manage that more easily than a man. Largely because the old myth still prevailed that we were the 'gentler sex', always kinder and nicer than the male of the species.

So a journalist would often request that I went with him. Sometimes, they'd actually brief me beforehand on what they wanted to get out of the interview. As I pottered around setting up my camera, I'd listen hard to the conversation and occasionally 'chip in' as casually as I could, steering the subject in the way I knew the reporter wanted it to go.

Working as a team like this was very much the method of the great French photo-magazine *Paris Match*, but it was far from the norm in Fleet Street. That was a shame because when it worked well, the results could be terrific. It could also work to the photographer's advantage because if the subject was opening up to the reporter, it often followed that this honesty would be reflected in their facial expression or the way they held their body. Making it far more likely that you'd be able to snatch that great 'picture', the look that somehow encapsulated what the story itself was all about.

Of course many photographers had no desire to 'chip in' at all and only wanted to concentrate on their 'art'. Nor did some journalists want a gobby photographer always butting in. But I loved being in a partnership. I found it stimulating and really enriching to my work. Luckily, I worked with some terrific *Mirror* journalists. Dear Marje of course, but also the feisty Anne Robinson, the great Christena Appleyard, Penny Vincenzi and Lesley Ebbetts. And, not least, my old chum from Paris days, Audrey Whiting, who'd returned to the *Mirror* and was now established as its Buckingham Palace correspondent. When she got the job, a joker commented it was because she was the only one who could see over the wall. Going out on a job with any of that lot really felt like 'girl-power', long before the term was invented.

Sometimes, I was even sent out with a half-decent bloke. The *Mirror* could boast an impressive list of male journalists too, such as Michael Grade, later of the BBC and Channel 4, and John Penrose, who was married to Anne Robinson. For many years, the grandly titled Royal Editor was the splendid James Whitaker, a jovial journalist of the old school, who was held in some affection by Princess Diana, although he'd revealed to the public that she suffered from the eating disorder bulimia. That was a story that got him into big trouble at the time, but which the Palace later admitted was true.

The *Mirror* was also home to two of the most admired journalists of the era. Paul Foot was a campaigning reporter, a staunch left-wing writer who also championed many causes célèbres, such as the case of the 'Birmingham Six'. John Pilger was our War Correspondent for twenty years, writing searing dispatches from Vietnam, Cambodia and many other war zones. Both Foot and Pilger were thorns in the side of the Establishment for their whole working lives. No other writers gave the *Mirror* more 'street cred'. Two extraordinary talents.

There was also a young man called Alastair Campbell, later to become famous as Tony Blair's 'spin doctor' and one of the most influential 'backroom boys' in Britain. Alistair and I used to get sent out together on what are known in the trade as vox pops. You go out on the street with a tape machine and a camera and ask the public their opinion on some issue or another. You know the sort of thing: 'Sharon Smith, aged twenty-four, poodle-clipper from Battersea, thinks Jim Davidson has gone too far again.' I found them a real drag, especially if it was cold and wet. But for some reason Alastair loved them.

'Oh, Doreen,' he used to say whenever I bumped into him. 'Those were the good old days. What fun we had.'

Well, I bloody didn't, but I did love the company of Alastair, a smashing guy and a brilliant reporter. Maybe this was when he first tuned in to how 'people in the street' spoke and thought, something that would be vital in his later career.

But I suppose it was always most fun to go out with a female reporter. Though not every job was some *Thelma and Louise* frolic. Far from it. Sometimes they were grim and distressing. When the Toxteth Riots broke out in Liverpool in 1981, Anne Robinson wanted to take a look, so she grabbed me and up we went. Toxteth had gone downhill badly since Anne's mother had run a market stall there many years before. Now it was a really deprived area. There had been several days of violent rioting, mostly by young black people against unfair police harassment, but also a cry of protest against the poverty and unemployment that was spreading across Britain in the wake of Margaret Thatcher's policies of running down the manufacturing industries.

The police had been attacked with petrol bombs and other missiles. Nearly five hundred of them, inadequately trained or equipped to deal with unrest on such a scale, were injured. They just hadn't known what had hit them. In retaliation, they'd used CS gas for the first time on mainland Britain. Hundreds of rioters were arrested. Shops were looted and cars burnt out. Scores of buildings were so badly damaged they had to be demolished. It was awful stuff. Annie and I stayed well clear of the violence but spent time talking to the young people who felt so dispossessed. There was such anger, it was scary. But such hopelessness too, which was just plain sad. I took photographs when I felt it was safe to do so. As a professional photographer, I knew that the images I'd captured were striking. For me, it was bloody depressing.

The Miners' Strike in the early Eighties was similarly bleak. But instead of a sudden outburst of rage in the hope of some better future, this was about people desperate to cling on to what little they had. It was a long, slow fight that crippled the lives of many of those caught in the heart of the conflict. Nearly 150,000 miners came out on strike, the biggest industrial dispute since the General Strike of 1926. The conflict lasted almost a year, during which time many miners' wives struggled to keep food on the table and clothes on the backs of their children. As a Labour paper, the *Mirror* was on the miners' side and sent me and a reporter to take a look at how they were coping. I couldn't believe what some of them were going through. When I got back home, I sent some clothing up to them. These women were valiant. There's no other word.

Our visit had needed to be approved by Arthur Scargill, the leader of the miners' union. To many people, Scargill was the devil incarnate. It's no exaggeration to say he was a man loathed by millions. Hitler with a Yorkshire accent. But he'd agreed to be photographed for our article. When I got to his house, half-drowned by sudden torrential rain, I was a bit early, but he pulled me inside and made me a nice cup of tea.

'Don't you dare go back and tell the *Mirror* I made you tea,' he said. 'They'll think I'm going soft.'

There wasn't much chance of anyone thinking that about our Arthur. It's a shame he imagined that being polite to a woman might somehow undermine his credibility. But there was a lot of silly macho posturing on both sides of that terrible struggle, while the wives and children went on suffering. In the end the miners lost and had to go back down the lift shafts to the coal faces, knowing that their days in work were numbered. When the strike started, there were nearly two hundred coal mines in Britain. Now there are only six and we import nearly all our coal.

When I travelled to Northern Ireland for a special feature, I saw a different sort of struggle, which had been going on for fifteen long years. It was a struggle in which several thousand had died, both in Ulster and in mainland Britain. Here again, there had been a lot of stubborn machismo on both sides and women had borne a heavy burden in trying to keep their homes and families functioning through it all. Many young adults could scarcely remember a life before it all started. In Belfast, especially along the Falls Road, I photographed some very desolate places and some equally exhausted faces, worn down by the endless years of The Troubles. From my selfish point of view, the giant murals painted on the gable-ends of many buildings made extraordinary images, sometimes of courage and defiance, but often of division and bigotry. At the time of my visit, it seemed that a solution would never be found and it would be almost another fifteen years before the Good Friday Agreement became the breakthrough that finally gave Northern Ireland hope for the future.

As a rule, I didn't often do 'hard news' stories, but I was sent to cover the 1987 Zeebrugge Ferry Disaster when a huge car ferry called the *Herald of Free Enterprise* capsized in the harbour of the Belgian port. Its bow doors had been left open when it set sail, causing it to tip over in little more than a minute. The ferry made an awful sight, lying on its side in the sea like some huge dead mammal. Nearly two hundred people were trapped inside the ship and died of hypothermia in the freezing water. It was the worse civilian maritime disaster since the end of the First World War.

Those who'd survived were taken into nearby Belgian hospitals. With their permission, the press was allowed in to hear their stories. I had to take pictures of these poor traumatised people, lying in their hospital beds, poleaxed by the horror that had befallen them. They'd gone off on a happy day-trip from Dover to the Continent and found themselves staring death in the face. Most of them owed their survival to no more than pure chance, whether they'd stayed on deck to get some air or gone below to buy a coffee. On such tiny decisions, our lives can hang. It was one of those difficult jobs when, despite permission, I felt deeply uncomfortable about being there at all.

But maybe the roughest assignment ever was a feature on the mothers of the girls killed by the Yorkshire Ripper. Over a period of years, Peter Sutcliffe had murdered thirteen young women across the north of England. A while after these awful events, some of their mothers agreed to let a newspaper into their homes. I'm not sure why, perhaps to try and rescue them from the lurid label of 'victim' and to restore them, in some small way, back to life. Despite these women's full agreement, the reporter and I felt we were treading on eggshells as we entered these sad houses, haunted by the awfulness of what had happened to the little girls who'd once lived and played in these rooms. I hope that I said the right things to them, but how on earth could you know what the right things could be?

As a mother of two young daughters, I couldn't begin to imagine how these desolate women had even begun to cope. They were all different of course. Some were reasonably resilient, others the walking wounded. I've never forgotten being shown the bedroom of one girl who'd been so viciously murdered. The single bed with the candlewick bedspread. The teddy bears on the pillow. The wallpaper a brilliant sunburst yellow, such a contrast to the darkness that had fallen on this house and on all the others. It was heartbreaking. When I got home, I was never so happy to find Jeanne and Catherine, now much the same age as the youngest victims, safe and sound. They both got an extra tight hug that night.

So although my life in Fleet Street was in many ways an escape from my troubles at home, it could never be an escape from 'life'. A tabloid newspaper needed to be, forgive the pun, a mirror that reflected every aspect of existence. Not just the movie stars and the pop singers nor the King's Road dolly birds in their miniskirts, but the dark and tragic side of life.

I've never forgotten being ordered out to cover a terrible fire in Fenchurch Street, not far from the office. That wasn't usually my sort of job, so maybe I was the only one available. When I arrived, the fire was at its height, an office building had turned into an inferno. Shouting and screaming. Fire engines everywhere, fat hoses pummelling the flames with water. There was a poor man who'd climbed out onto a window ledge and was clinging onto a drain-pipe, which was probably red-hot. A ladder was almost within his reach but not quite. People on an adjacent roof-top were encouraging him to make the leap for the ladder. The smoke and flames seemed to get worse by the minute. I took my photographs with my heart racing. No doubt, he'd been just like me this morning. Got up, had breakfast, said goodbye to his wife and kids, maybe come in on a train from some quiet suburb, just as I had done. And now this. By the time he fell to his death, I was gone. I certainly couldn't have tried to capture his final moments.

Unlike many brave professionals, I could never have photographed the worst horrors that life might bring. The great war photographers like Robert Capa and Don McCullin didn't flinch from graphic snapshots of death and destruction. I don't think I could have handled the aftermath of the Aberfan disaster, as Pierre had tried to do and failed. I don't believe this was because of being a woman as such; there were plenty of male photographers who couldn't have done either. Nor was I afraid of capturing the bleaker side of life. I just needed to deal with it in a less immediate way.

In 2016, there was a major commemoration on the centenary of The Battle of the Somme. Half a century ago, I covered the fiftieth anniversary of that terrible event, a battle that lasted five months and in which well over a million lives were lost on both sides. At that time, there were still a fair number of survivors alive. I talked to many of these men, by then mostly in their seventies and eighties. Most wore dark blazers, awash with ribbons and medals; forty-two Victoria Crosses had been won at the Somme. They told me their tales of those awful months and how they'd managed to get through. It was humbling to hear. The plains around the River Somme were still and beautiful on a warm July day. It was almost impossible to imagine the horror that had taken place there. Only the endless rows of tombstones told the story.

Some of these elderly men began to feel the summer heat and took off their jackets to stand around in shirts and braces. But most, no matter how hot it got, were never going to take off their blazer. Those medals that sparkled on their chests meant more to them than anything. They were charmers to a man. They had seen terrible atrocities, worse than most of us could ever imagine, but they had somehow kept their humanity intact. On the very ground where they might have been cut down, they still stood tall, even if now they were a little stooped. What might have been a miserable, traumatic place was instead an uplifting and hopeful one.

Being sucked into the sadness of Zeebrugge, the Somme, Toxteth and the Miner's Strike taught you things, not just about other people, but also about yourself. It helped you to value what you had, however imperfect it might have been. In my case, a poor mother with clinical depression and a husband who drank to ease his unhappiness. It also helped you understand people's weakness and vulnerability as well as their strengths and the joy they could bring you. And I like to think it made me a more sympathetic person.

Anyway, there was no choice. It was all part of the job. The *Daily Mirror* was a mass-market paper, a paper for ordinary folk. Events like those above were all about such people, people who'd been caught up in something bigger than themselves. All these stories reflected our mission as a newspaper and I was very, very proud of that.

Chapter Eleven

Shooting Stars

'Do you want Mum to give up work?'

The day finally came when I sat the three of them down on a sofa and asked the question. I'd been thinking about asking it for a long time. Tony was in his teens now, the girls a bit younger but already at the age where they were obsessed by pop groups and film stars.

'Why?' asked one of them. 'Don't you like doing it anymore?'

'Yes, but I just thought you might be fed up with me being out of the house so much. Getting home late. That sort of thing.'

'We don't mind,' said another.

'So you wouldn't want me to pack it in and be here all the time?'

The same look crossed all three of those faces. It wasn't exactly horror, but it was certainly alarm.

'No! We like hearing about the people you take photos of. We tell all our friends at school.'

'Yeah, nobody else's mum does anything like you do.'

The penny dropped. Daft of me not to have realised. If anyone thinks the cult of celebrity is a new phenomenon, they're wrong. You've only got to look at footage of Beatlemania to know that. Or all the knickers thrown at Tom Jones, enough to open a new branch of Marks & Spencer. Teenage girls, including me, have been daft since the year dot.

By this point in our lives, there was enough in the kitty for me either to have stopped working or at least gone freelance so I could spend a bit more time at home. Pierre was still making some money as a freelance too. We'd have got by. If it was going to improve the quality of our family life, bring us closer together, I'd have done it.

But even on that first evening in 1962 when I'd got home after my return to the *Mirror*, I'd seen that my kids would deal with having a working mother. I'd never been quite sure how much of that was a performance, putting a brave face on it. They still came to meet me off the train. Arms were still flung around me. Over the years, I'd tried to keep a sharp eye on them, looking for any sign that my not being there was affecting them in any serious way. Both Jeanne and Catherine seemed fine, but there were possible hints of it in Tony. He'd always been a bit of a tearaway and always would be. Was that down to an absentee mother?

But the unanimous decision from the sofa was that Mum should go on working. For the simple, silly reason that their mother was, however indirectly, a bit glamorous.

There's no denying that some of my work did merit that adjective. I certainly had brief encounters with so many famous names that I've forgotten half of them. That sounds blasé, but I often only spent an hour or so in their starry company and I sometimes forgot them as quickly as they certainly forgot me.

Naturally, you had to learn how to handle celebrities. Very often these were big egos you were dealing with, however pleasant they might be on the surface (or not). They were people used to approval and deference.

Some were incredibly vain, like the Duchess of Windsor, terrified the lens might expose the rings on her bark. Others, like the French actress Simone Signoret, married to the gorgeous Yves Montand, were just the opposite.

'Come on, Doreen, get closer,' she said. ''I've earned every one of these wrinkles and I'm proud of them.'

Good on you, Simone. She'd once been exceptionally beautiful but now that she no longer was, she didn't give a damn. The Greek actress and politician Melina Mercouri, the star of *Never on Sunday*, was the same. Both were down-to-earth European women, sure of themselves, unafraid to face up to the ticking of the clock. Unlike the American Duchess who'd never been good-looking in the first place and who was petrified of losing what few charms she had. Maybe a psychologist could work all that out.

It wasn't just the ladies who could be vain. Freddie Mercury was a prime example of the peacock male. He was a great showman. No camera scared him, he loved posing. He was a beautiful-looking man, incredible cheekbones you could've hung your washing on. I photographed him in the Seventies when he still wore that haircut which made men look like medieval pageboys. He appeared in a stunning blue-and-white satin costume with matching high heels. He strutted into the studio on his daft heels and promptly fell over, flat on his face. But Freddie's feathers were totally unruffled. He just picked himself up and went on strutting. He was ego personified, but had that star quality that let him get away with it.

So did the pianist Liberace who, in terms of sparkle and glitter, made Freddie Mercury look like your maiden aunt. At his peak, Liberace was the highest-paid entertainer in the world. Over-the-top didn't begin to describe him. He was often driven onto the stage in a white Rolls-Royce. His stage costumes, floor-length mink coats on top of jewel-encrusted suits, capes made of pink feathers, were sensational. Nearly every finger carried a huge jewelled ring. Long before my time, he'd once sued the *Daily Mirror* for an article that implied he was gay. He'd actually won the case which, in the light of later revelations, seems incredible. Luckily for me, he'd not banned the paper from the photo-call at the London Palladium where I photographed him. Despite the sentimental, sugary façade, he was, in his own way, totally genuine. Behind the candelabra, there was a great warmth and humanity about him that was tangible and which I tried to catch in my pictures. He just loved to entertain people and make them happy. Not much wrong with that. Even if he wasn't your cup of tea, he was definitely a class act.

For a photographer, the worst scenario was the grumpy sitter who'd been dragged kicking and screaming towards your lens.

When I was sent to photograph Sophia Loren at the Savoy Hotel, I knew in a second that she would rather have been anywhere else. She never cracked a smile once. Mind you, she had a lot on her mind. At that time, the Italian tax authorities were chasing her over an alleged unpaid bill and she would later spend a few days in jail. Possibly though, she was just plain bored out of her skull, having spent half her life doing this. When that happens, all you can do is be diplomatic and try to ease them gently into it. Not make too many demands too quickly. I've seen some photographers be far too assertive, then the subject throws a tantrum and walks off in a huff. So you have to recognise which way the wind is blowing and bend with it.

In the end, a pissed-off Miss Loren looked even more beautiful than a chirpy, smiling one would have done. I put her on the window seat to look wistfully out over the Thames and the pictures were fine. But there was a definite sense of a smouldering volcano, so I did the job and got the hell out of there before she erupted and threw a plate of spaghetti.

Paul McCartney wasn't a happy little soldier either. I photographed him and his first wife, Linda, in a rowing boat on a lake. Can't remember why now. Just the three of us, marooned together. No escape. He was perfectly polite, but I had the feeling he'd liked to have thrown me overboard. I think I even did the rowing. The same went for Yoko Ono and her son, Sean Lennon. A strange experience. One of those sessions that was like pulling teeth. Maybe I wasn't as famous as Annie Leibovitz and they felt they were slumming. God knows.

It was never very pleasant if I sensed that a celebrity really hated my being there. But I made myself remember that these people had entered into a sort of pact with the media. The careers they had chosen for themselves and out of which many of them had made pots of money, were based on talent but, in many cases at least, it could be kept alive long past its sell-by date with the oxygen of publicity. No pictures, no features in the newspapers and those careers could fade quite quickly. That was true then and it's a hundred times more true today.

But the delightful ones could make up for all the grumpiness you sometimes had to face. The two chat-show kings, Terry Wogan and Michael Parkinson, were always sunny and welcoming. When you went to the BBC, there was always tight security. Your credentials were carefully checked, then you were led through endless corridors by production assistants towards the inner sanctum. But when you reached Parky, all that stuff was swept away with a big smile.

'You don't need to introduce me to Doreen,' he'd always say. 'I know her.'

With both the Yorkshireman and the Irishman what you saw on screen, you got in life.

It was the same with Stéphane Grappelli, the jazz violinist who became hugely popular in Britain and made people totally rethink the slightly stuffy image of that instrument. A delightful man. I got him to sit on a bench in Soho Square with his fiddle so that he looked like an old busker down on his luck, instead of one of the great violinists of his time. The incongruity of it worked a treat, what Freddie Reed would have called a 'picture'.

And I'll never forget the lovely Marty Feldman, a great comedian who died much too young. Such an amazing face to photograph. It was right up there with Albert Einstein. That curly hair and those bulging eyes, which unfortunately not only bulged but crossed.

'Marty, would you mind looking at the camera?'

'What do you mean, Doreen? I am looking at the bleeding

camera!'

Another star who died much too soon was Lynda Bellingham, the fine actress also known as the 'Oxo Mum' of the long-running TV commercials. She'd not had an easy life but it hadn't left her bitter or twisted. She had a warm, winning personality that my camera had no trouble picking up. Never sulky, never a diva. Always ready to give you her best. I once admired a pretty lamp in her house and she tried her best to make me have it. When I read she was terminally ill, I wanted to write to her and send her my good wishes. But I felt it might be intrusive and I didn't. Now of course I wish I had. Maybe my letter would have brightened her day, even for a minute. How daft we are sometimes. There aren't always second chances.

Some celebrities who were totally relaxed in front of a TV or movie camera could be petrified by the sight of a stills camera. Often these were actors, who were totally comfortable when playing a part, but nervous as kittens without a role to hide behind. Pauline Quirke and Linda Robson in the early days of their huge success with *Birds of a Feather* had never been inside a photographic studio before.

'Oh, Doreen, love, what for heaven's sake do we do?'

'Just be yourselves, girls,' I replied.

'Oh, Gawd, how do we do that?'

But they managed it, the pictures were great and I'd never had so many laughs in the space of an hour.

But some of the very best pictures were the darker ones, where the sitter was unhappy and didn't feel the need to hide it.

The great comedian Les Dawson had not long lost his wife when I photographed him in his dressing room at a theatre up north. He had an extraordinary face, which he was able to twist into grotesque shapes, because he'd broken his jaw in a boxing match. He didn't pull any funny faces for my camera that night, just stared at me and let me capture everything he was feeling. Then, despite his own troubles, he put on his make-up, went out

SCOOP! It was "hold the front page" when innocent-looking "office girl" Doreen managed to capture the picture that all of Fleet Street was after. The two young women at the heart of the court case of the century, Christine Keeler and Mandy Rice-Davies, having a quiet drink in a candid camera shot that was secured from the ladies' loo!

IT'S A HARD-KNOCK LIFE

Editorial meetings at the Daily Mirror (above right) were always looking for impactful stories – and photographs.

A 'working girl' from Shepherd Market, Mayfair (above left), spoke as part of a ground-breaking series on "Women Talking".

Beryl Leach (right), mother of Yorkshire Ripper victim Barbara, in her daughter's bedroom in Kettering, in 1981.

Dockers (left) wait in the early morning in 1965, for work to be allocated to their specific gangs.

Miners' wives during the 1984 strike (right) photographed outside a community centre where local women provided lunches three days a week

PEOPLE IN CRISIS

A survivor of the Herald of Free Enterprise ferry disaster at Zeebrugge sorts through clothes looking for something to wear (above left).

The natural exuberance of children makes a playground even of Ulster during The Troubles (above right), with gestures mirroring the extraordinary gable-end murals.

Women bar the way (left), protesting against the siting of US nuclear weapons at Greenham Common.

Poor mothers in India (right), where Doreen spent a month, and found herself inspired and overwhelmed by the whole experience – "an assault on the senses"

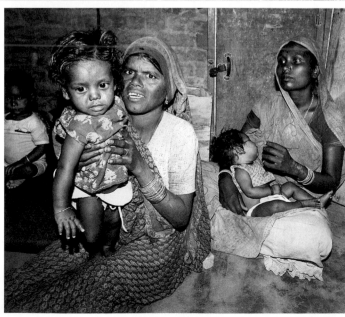

AND THEY CALL THIS GLAMOUR!

Doreen (above left) learned to survive a certain 'laddishness' from her Mirror colleagues back in those chauvinist days. And, on assignments, she was the hard-working invisible woman behind many of the paper's "glamour" shots (above right).

Perennial favourite Jilly Johnson (right) goes topless and bottomless – that bikini is painted on!

A more basic approach to headwear for Doreen working at Ascot (above).

Capturing a Paris showgirl (left) getting ready to go on stage at Le Lido, 1980

on the stage and brought joy to a thousand people. The same
with another comedian, Mike Reid, who was also famous for his
role as Frank Butcher in *EastEnders*. He'd been through the wars
a few times and it showed. He often played Cockney gangster
roles, which that rough-hewn face suited perfectly, but anyone
could see the serious, highly sensitive actor behind it. The
sadness behind the laughter of the clown is an awful cliché, but it
was so often true.

One of the few times I did feel seriously glam was when I
photographed the author Harold Robbins in St Tropez. He loved
to personify the hedonistic macho lifestyle he wrote about in books
such as *The Carpetbaggers* and *The Adventurers*. Apparently, he'd sold
a total of 750 million books in his career. They weren't my cup of
tea. They were bloke's books really, all guns and nipples. He
insisted that the pictures were done on his glittering yacht. He also
insisted that the yacht sailed round the bay while they were taken.
God knows why. It made no difference to me.

I think Harold was one of those occasional subjects who're
tickled pink by the sight of a woman behind a camera. I somehow
sensed that a male photographer wouldn't have been invited
aboard. But I was far from being the only female on deck. A bevy
of sexy girls in bikinis, like characters out of his novels, were
draped across the deck. I imagined they had names like Topaz or
Amethyst. Their main function seemed to be to prop up Harold's
notorious image as a playboy. Sadly, I wasn't invited to join
Harold's harem, I doubt a mother of three from south London
called Doreen was quite his type. St Tropez was rather nice
though, and it was a bit of a shock to be back on the train into
Holborn Viaduct the very next morning, going up through
Catford and Lewisham.

But even Harold Robbins' yacht couldn't quite beat being sent
to the Bahamas with Spandau Ballet. They were making an
album in a recording studio out there and the *Mirror* was going to
promote it. My daughters were mad with envy. I spent a very nice

week photographing pretty boys in their swimming trunks, cavorting around on the golden sands – one of those jobs when it was hard to believe you were actually getting paid. They were sweet boys, especially Tony Hadley. Co-operative, no bother at all. Very unlike the first time we'd met, when they'd started kicking a football around the *Mirror* studio. I tolerated it for about two minutes before I screamed at them. That shut them up. Sometimes being a mother of stroppy teenagers had its professional uses. I guess when they saw me in the Bahamas, they thought, 'Oh, god, it's that old bag again,' and were on their best behaviour.

None of these people were trained for the camera. You always had to make allowances for that and, as I've said, gently coax out of them what you wanted without ever being a bully. Not always easy.

By contrast, it was always a joy to work with those who had been schooled to perform. Ballet dancers were prime examples of this. They knew instinctively how to 'strike a pose', place their body in a position that would make a great picture. Whenever I got called to go to the Royal Opera House, Covent Garden, I knew I'd come back with some striking images.

Shooting Rudolf Nureyev and Margot Fonteyn was a dream. They were exquisite together. Poetry in motion is a corny expression, but that's what they were. Fonteyn was almost twenty years older than Nureyev the Russian firebrand. But you'd never have guessed it onstage. She could make you believe anything she wanted, a gift that the great classical dancers, actors and singers always possess. Though Nureyev was essentially gay, rumour had it that he and Fonteyn had briefly been lovers. I'd not have been surprised if that were true. Their devotion to each other showed through in every step they danced.

But my favourite ballet shot was of two oldies, Sir Robert Helpmann and Sir Frederick Ashton, when they danced the Ugly Sisters in *Cinderella*. Grotesque and endearing at the same time, they looked almost pathetic beside the porcelain beauty of Margot

Fonteyn. Years before, Helpmann had been the young Fonteyn's regular partner at the beginning of her career. Ballet is a tough world. I wondered if these two great male dancers found it difficult that the passing of time had edged them into such character roles. Even if they did, they still stole the show.

Torvill and Dean, the Olympic ice-skating champions, had the same balletic gift. Almost every time they turned their bodies they gave you yet another beautiful image. And they were such a nice unspoiled pair of young people. Just ordinary kids who'd discovered they possessed a quite extraordinary gift.

Olga Korbut also had a degree of control over her body which made her a joy to photograph. The famous Russian gymnast was a girl of eighteen when I first met her but, being less than five-foot tall, looked very much younger. 'The Sparrow from Minsk' had won four Gold medals at the 1972 Olympics and become an instant celebrity all over the world. In those days, at the height of the Cold War, the Soviet Union seemed an alien, frightening place to many people in the West and not without reason. The bubbly, open-hearted Olga was a public relations godsend to the Russians, the polar opposite of everything we perceived that country to be.

The *Daily Mirror* was going to sponsor Olga's appearance at Earl's Court in London, so I'd been sent to Moscow in advance to do photographs and publicise the event. She spoke reasonable English and we got along at once. She'd been trained as a gymnast since the age of nine and was watched over every minute by her trainers and her Soviet minders. I went to watch her train and was horrified to see the poor kid crying from exhaustion as they ground her down. She'd already achieved so much for Mother Russia, but they always wanted more. Only perfection was acceptable, human frailty wasn't on their radar. They tried to control her like a puppet, but Olga had a spirit they couldn't entirely conquer.

We were staying in the same hotel and Olga had wanted to come up to see my room, but that was strictly forbidden. God knows what they imagined I might do to her. Indoctrinate her with capitalist propaganda maybe. Or show her my photos of Showaddywaddy or other 'degenerates'.

But when she eventually arrived in London for her show, I became a sort of mother substitute. We went to Number 10 Downing Street, to meet the Prime Minister, Edward Heath. Dear old Ted wasn't the most charismatic of men, not exactly Robert Redford, and little Olga was less than enthralled. By now though, she had the impression that I was some sort of fairy godmother who could wave a magic wand and open all doors.

'Doreen, there is one place I really wish to go, please,' she said.

'Yes, dear, where's that?'

'I wish to go to Buckingham Palace and meet the Queen.'

'Ooh, I'm not sure I can manage that, dear.'

'Why not, Doreen? Are you not a very important woman here in England?'

'I wouldn't say that, dear.'

'Oh.'

I took many pictures of Olga performing. She really was astonishing. But most were lost when a fire burnt down the storage facility in which the *Mirror* kept much of its photographic archive. Hey ho…

I never saw Olga again after that. In later years she became a coach herself and eventually moved to America, where she married and had children. She's still one of the most revered heroines in sport. Despite the pressure she endured, she seems to have coped and has had a happy adult life. I'm really glad to know that. She was a fine person and I was proud to be her surrogate mum, if only for a while.

There are striking parallels between Olga Korbut and another tiny girl whose gigantic talent dragged her into the spotlight when she should really have been playing with her dolls. At the age of ten, a little Scottish singer called Lena Zavaroni won a TV contest called *Opportunity Knocks* (the *X Factor* of its day). She became, and still remains, the youngest person ever to have a solo album in the UK charts. She performed before the Queen and appeared on American TV with Frank Sinatra. But the simple kid who loved to sing was by now on the treadmill of recordings, concerts, TV shows. She was a 'product' and other people were making a lot of money from her. Maybe that's acceptable for an adult but it's fraught with danger for a child. By the time she was thirteen, Lena had begun a battle with anorexia nervosa, the eating disorder. Her career faded, though there were frequent comebacks, which never lasted long. She got married but that didn't last long either. She was dead by the age of thirty-five.

The photographs I took in her teens show it all. A nice girl, she was trying to do her best for me. In some shots, she gave me a lovely smile, but in others, those huge eyes in her thin face looked so sad. One of the pictures was sadly ironic, showing her cheerfully putting coins into a machine that dispensed chocolate bars. If only she'd been as relaxed and carefree about such things as she looked in the photograph. That day, posing for me was probably just another turn of the treadmill on which she was trapped and I'm sorry for that.

The life of a child star, in whatever context, is a risky one. Some make it through, others don't. Olga Korbut did, Lena Zavaroni didn't. I've never been sorry that none of my three children ever found themselves in that kind of spotlight. It can burn people up. People often say that the Page Three models were exploited, though the girls themselves claimed they never felt that. Perhaps it was the Olgas and the Lenas who were used in a much more destructive way.

So the glamorous life that my kids believed I led wasn't always a bed of roses. But I usually felt I was photographing somebody who, even if I didn't like them much, at least deserved to be well-known. They'd done something to merit their fame. I don't think I'd much enjoy shooting some of the nonentities who pass as celebrities these days. No thanks very much.

One last tip if you're going to photograph a celeb. Try not to kill them. I went to the London Palladium to photograph Danny Kaye, the great American entertainer, then at the height of his worldwide fame. His season at the Palladium had been a sensation. King George VI, Queen Elizabeth and the two princesses had, for the first time ever, abandoned the royal box for seats in the front row.

He was a charmer was Danny. One of the 'old school' who appreciated how important the press was to their career and who would never have been rude to any reporter or photographer. It was back in the days when we still used cumbersome cameras and handheld flash guns. It was just Danny and me in the dressing room. It was hot and cramped and I had to stand close to him to get the pic.

When I triggered the flash, it exploded, sending tiny fragments of glass all over him. In his hair, over his clothes. Miraculously, he wasn't blinded, not even cut. But it could have scarred him for life. I was horrified, but Danny Kaye was sweet. He just brushed it off, literally and metaphorically. These days, a celeb would probably have slapped a multi-million-dollar lawsuit on me and the paper. Danny Kaye was a star with style, though what he said about me afterwards, I shudder to think. I pictured the headline that might have been: 'Danny Kaye dies. *Mirror* photographer gets exclusive picture.'

Apart from such occasional disasters, I was generally regarded as a competent photographer. I was always chuffed when people sometimes appreciated my work. I was already a Fellow of the British Institute of Press Photographers but Freddie Reed, the royal photographer, the 'father' of us all at the *Mirror*, had encouraged me to put my work forward for a fellowship of the Royal Photographic Society. In the photographic world, this was Mount Everest and Becher's Brook rolled into one. And what d'you know, I got it. I was pleased as punch. Pierre said all the right things, whatever his private feelings might have been. My

Dad was ecstatic. Mum was too, without quite understanding its significance. But a few of the 'boys' in the photographers' room were a bit nonplussed, though in the nicest possible way.

'Crikey, Doreen, how did you swing that then?'

Male pride was stirred and I reckon a few portfolios were secretly put together and sent off to the Royal Photographic Society before you could say 'green-eyed monster'.

On the big day, I received my award alongside Lord Snowdon, then still married to Princess Margaret. He was a delightful man, no airs and graces at all. It was a thrill to be recognised alongside Snowdon, not because of the royal connection, but because he was such a tremendous photographer, not just for his portraits of the rich and famous, but also of deprived inner city life and of the disabled and mentally ill. Snowdon's work usually appeared in such upmarket organs as *The Sunday Times* and *Vogue*, but if he had any reservations about getting his FRPS beside some bird from the *Daily Mirror*, he never let it show.

An article duly appeared in the paper with the unavoidable headline 'For she's a jolly good Fellow!' The tabloids never could resist a pun.

Chapter Twelve

Girls on Film

'You don't mind getting your kit off for Doreen,' she said. 'It's like stripping in front of your Granny.'

None of the photographers at the *Daily Mirror* was exactly ecstatic about the introduction of the now infamous Page Three. But we accepted that it was almost inevitable. *The Sun* had started it and their circulation had climbed at the expense of our own. And so it began.

Since the Sixties, we'd always done what were called 'glamour' shots. In America they were known as 'cheesecake'. Scantily clad girls, usually in bikinis or sexy lingerie, but well this side of decency. You might say they derived from the *Carry On* school of sexiness – Barbara Windsor with her bra flying off. A bit seaside-postcard. Saucy rather than erotic. I'd done tons of glamour pictures. I'd never found them very interesting to do, it was just part of the working day. They certainly weren't very challenging for a photographer.

But then glamour morphed into topless. Nowadays, these pictures are regarded as almost a 'crime' against the female race, but it really didn't seem that way at the time. Maybe you have to judge everything in the context of the age. The cultural 'revolution' of the Sixties hadn't just been about fashion and pop music. It had been a sexual revolution too. Columnists like Marje Proops had played a big part in that, encouraging their readers to no longer be embarrassed or hesitant about taking pleasure in sex. It was all part of blowing those post-war cobwebs away. For so long, the pendulum had been fixed at the repressed, inhibited end of things that, when it finally swung, it swung all the way to the opposite side.

The Sun, a successor to the old *Daily Herald* on which my Dad had once worked, had been launched in 1964 but had not been a success. It had been on its last legs when an Australian media tycoon called Rupert Murdoch bought it from IPC (who also owned the *Mirror*) in 1969. The revamped paper had made a brash, noisy entrance into Fleet Street and soon had a good circulation. As a mass-market tabloid, it was in direct competition with the *Mirror* though a lot more downmarket. It introduced its first bare breast, though very discreetly, in 1970 and, over the next few years, the photographs became increasingly bold until there was nothing remotely discreet about them.

From the start there were loud protests that these pictures were demeaning to women. After all, this was the time of the birth of what became called 'feminism' and the very same year that Germaine Greer's *The Female Eunuch* was flying off the bookshelves. But those protests weren't going to stop the newspaper bosses of Fleet Street from using Page Three to fight a circulation war. And compared to what was shown in the 'lad mags' like *Playboy*, *Penthouse* and *Mayfair*, the newspaper pictures were relatively tame.

And so my 'boys' and I began to do them. Poor Arthur Sidey, the animal photographer, loathed it. He had no problem with shooting a gorilla's tits but hated snapping a real live woman's. None of us much enjoyed it.

The only ones who seemed to enjoy it much were the models. Women like Samantha Fox, Linda Lusardi and Jilly Johnson were all cheerful girls, proud of their lovely young bodies, who didn't find it degrading in the least. They knew their careers would be short and wanted to make the most of their celebrity and the very good money they were earning. These were the girls who'd grown up in the Swinging Sixties. Unlike their mothers, they didn't find nudity shameful in any way. The very opposite in fact. And if you'd told them they were being exploited, they'd have thought you were nuts.

With topless shots, I always took the same approach that I had with the fashion shots I'd done with Felicity Green. Happy, fun, filled with the joy of being young and pretty. Never seedy or sleazy. And just because somebody has their clothes off doesn't make them sexy. In my opinion, it was the expression on the face that made a picture sexy or not. Mind you, I did so many of these shots that no doubt the rumours I was a lesbian surfaced again.

But time passes and moods change. Everything evolves. As the years went by, the feminist way of thinking dripped more and more into the consciousness of most women and of an increasing number of men too. More and more voices were raised against Page Three and, in the mid-Eighties, the *Daily Mirror* announced that it would publish no more topless shots, the first tabloid to take that stance.

The now reviled Page Three was a phenomenon of its time. That time has passed and is not mourned. To everything there is a season.

And so, at the *Mirror* at least, the bikini tops went back on. In the photographers' room, nobody was sorry. But we still featured pretty girls to please the readership. The *Mirror*, like all newspapers, often got requests for prints of pictures that readers had particularly liked. Sometimes they'd be addressed directly to me. Very often these came from prisoners in Britain's jails.

'Dear Doreen Spooner, any chance you could send me a copy of the photo of that bird Linda Lusardi in today's paper? It'd be nice to have it on the wall of the cell. She's got a look of my old mum. All the best etc..'

We would always oblige. It was also interesting to notice that once the topless photographs stopped, the number of requests didn't decline that much. My nicest shot of Samantha Fox showed her scrubbed of make-up, fully clothed and with the gentle smile that reflected her sweet personality. Maybe that says it all. And though my photographs hadn't yet made it into the National Portrait Gallery, it was good to know they'd been widely exhibited on the walls of Pentonville, Wandsworth and Wormwood Scrubs.

After Page Three was extinct, some wonderful young models passed in front of my lens. Jerry Hall, six feet high, had a fabulous heart-shaped face and that outgoing American spirit that the camera always loves. Catherine Zeta-Jones, the future Oscar-winning star of *Chicago* but then just a dancer in the musical *42nd Street*, was a stunning girl and a warm, delightful person. In Heather Mills, before the accident that cost her a leg, you could easily see the spirit that would later help her deal with that tragedy. Jerry later married Mick Jagger and, just recently, Rupert Murdoch. Catherine wed the actor Michael Douglas and Heather bagged Paul McCartney, at least for a while. The tradition of rich and famous men marrying gorgeous models is as old as the hills and will seemingly never end. At the time of writing, Mrs Donald Trump stands a chance of being the next First Lady of the United States. It's amazing where the catwalk can lead you.

Anyway, at least the *Mirror* did something to atone for its 'crime' by introducing a new series called 'Page Three Fella. I had a very nice time snapping hunky blokes in their swimming trunks for the delectation of British women (and possibly men too, of course). I fairly scampered into the studio on those days. Perhaps my obvious enjoyment of these shoots finally laid to rest the rumours that I might be a lesbian. Sadly, these young gods no doubt saw me as their 'granny' too. But it was fun to imagine women all over Britain looking forward to their daily dose of chiselled abs and glistening pecs.

'Phwoar, Sandra, look at the tits on that.'

But, as a photographer, it was far more interesting to chronicle the things that were happening to women with their clothes on.

148

'Women Talking' was a series of features on the lives of 'ordinary' British women all over the country. Rich and poor, black and white. With Christena Appleyard, who was a terrific, sensitive reporter, I went the length and breadth of the country to get their stories.

We went to a convent to interview a young nun. She was nothing like the stereotype at all. She told us how much she and her fellow nuns still liked the sight of a handsome man. 'We're still women after all.' Yes of course they were. How stupid of the rest of us to imagine otherwise. She talked about the pain she'd caused her family by shutting herself away. She was such a brave girl. How strong her faith must have been, how sure of the path she'd taken.

We went into the alleyways of Shepherd Market in London's Mayfair in search of a prostitute. I'd thought it might be hard to find girls willing to talk to us, but not at all. Nor did they have any problem with their real names being used. There was no embarrassment or shame about what they did for a living. I found the same thing when I did a later feature in a French brothel. It was a tough world and they had to find a way to survive. Why should they be ashamed?

In stark contrast, we went to a fabulous flat in Cadogan Square, Chelsea, to feature the debutante daughter of the famous actress Moira Lister, who in private life was married to a French viscount. It was courageous of the girl to admit the leftie *Daily Mirror* into her home when her natural habitat was *Tatler* and *Country Life*. I wondered why she'd done it. We might well have done a hatchet job, but we didn't, although her lifestyle was certainly on a different planet from that of nearly all our readers. But even in those times, of CND, a Labour government and the established order mocked and attacked as never before, there was still an endless fascination with the rich and titled. Has it gone away? Of course not. It's stronger than ever. Oh well...

We went to a confectionery factory in Pontefract, Yorkshire. All day long, five-and-a-half days a week, the women on the production line produced pipes made of liquorice for the schoolkids of Britain. The smell of the liquorice was overpowering, the heat and the noise awful, but the sheer boredom was unimaginable. How they stayed sane, I can't imagine. I was so grateful for the diversity and excitement of my own work. I wondered how the young lady in Cadogan Square would have coped in Pontefract.

I was proud of my photographs for Women Talking. Women's voices were being increasingly heard and it was hardly before time. Fascinating, sobering, entertaining.

The series was so popular that we even extended it abroad. With Anne Robinson, I spent a hair-raising month in India, investigating the lives of women there. Nothing quite prepares you for India. It is nothing less than an assault on the senses. The colours, the smells, the noise, the sheer overwhelming crush of humanity. For a photographer, it was like being in a sweetie-shop. Every way your head turned, another image begged to be captured.

But it was almost impossible to adjust to the grinding poverty all around you. I'd never seen anything like it. The gap between the rich and the poor was vast. We went to some of the poorest areas and saw the working and living conditions that women were coping with. On a building site, I photographed female labourers with piles of bricks stacked on their heads in the way that models do with books to improve their posture. Heaven knows what effect such weight had on their heads and bodies. I promised myself to stop moaning about the weight of my cameras. I saw a simple infant school, little more than a shack, where the children learnt their lessons sitting in the dirt. There were beggars, often hideously disabled, on every street corner.

In glaring contrast, the lives of the wealthy were unimaginably opulent. Anne and I were invited into the palace of a maharaja, crammed with exquisite objects, any one of which would have fed a poor family for a year. The aristocrats were extremely nice, very Anglicised, their smallest whim obeyed by a small regiment of servants. If they were troubled by the horrendous inequalities of their enormous country, they certainly never mentioned it. Possibly they felt that was how it had always been and always would be.

It was a fascinating trip, but a real eye-opener. Britain, so much less colourful and with its lousy climate, suddenly seemed like a kind of paradise. At least we had the Welfare State, designed to try and stop people sinking below a certain level. But the poverty and suffering here was heartbreaking.

There were some lighter moments though. One night I was asleep in my hotel room when the phone rang. It was Anne Robinson in a terrible flap.

'Doreen, Doreen, there's a rat running around my bedroom! What shall I do?'

'What the hell are you ringing me for?' I asked. 'Call the bloody manager or clobber it yourself.'

Anne Robinson was a fine journalist and good fun to work with. By the time she came to the *Mirror*, she'd already had a turbulent life, having married, divorced and lost the custody of her young daughter because of her alcoholism. But she'd now managed to stop drinking and was well on the road to the spectacular career that would culminate in *The Weakest Link*, a job that would earn her the title of 'Queen of Mean'. But even in her *Mirror* days, she was laying the foundations of that acerbic persona in a weekly column called The Wednesday Witch. She was a tough cookie and no mistake. She'd certainly never have got a job in the Diplomatic Corps. Sometimes on an assignment, I'd hear her be pretty rough on people.

'What on earth did you speak to him like that for?' I'd ask.

'What do you mean?'

'Did you have to be quite so rude?' I'd snap back. 'For God's sake, Annie, lighten up.'

That night in India, I was daft enough to go to her room to see what was happening. While Annie stood trembling in a corner, a poor Indian hotel manager, armed with a broom and sweating like a pig, chased the rat around the room. If only I'd taken my camera, I could be blackmailing her to this day. She's really not as tough as she pretends to be. I can't now remember what happened to the rat, but one thing was certain. If he'd known it was Anne Robinson's room, he'd never have dared.

But one other famous lady was every bit as fierce as her image. When it came to 'Women Talking', nobody talked louder than her. So loud that she'll probably be heard down the centuries to come. I've clean forgotten now why Margaret Thatcher invited a Labour newspaper into Number 10 Downing Street. Knowing her, there must have been one. Maybe she was hoping for a mass conversion of Labour voters. I climbed the famous stairs where framed pictures of previous prime ministers climbed up the walls alongside me. I wondered if the effect was supposed to suggest that, at the top of the stairs, up on Mount Olympus, I was going to meet the greatest of them all.

When I got there, it didn't feel that way. Maybe she was used to photographers with lots of gear, whereas I'd decided to bring just one light camera. If she was pleased to encounter a female behind the lens, she certainly didn't show it.

'You have fifteen minutes, Miss Spooner.'

She was bloody difficult. She didn't want to pose at all. She expected me to scuttle around her while she read her papers from the famous red boxes. So that's what I did and then, as with Sophia Loren, got the hell out of there. When that's the score, it's the only thing to do. The results were passable, no more. When the subject won't engage with you, you have to switch to the Cartier-Bresson route and hope that a shot taken unawares will, by some miracle, give you that 'picture'. But not this time.

Among the many criticisms of the 'Iron Lady' was that she did very little to further the rights of women. She'd undoubtedly broken through a political glass ceiling and made history, which was no mean achievement. But that was about it. As with Marje Proops, Felicity Green, Anne Robinson and even with me, the cliché was that we were women who'd made it in 'a man's world'. With Margaret Thatcher, I'm not sure she even acknowledged there was such a thing as a 'man's world'. She just knew what she wanted and went out there and got it. Impressive, just not much help to the rest of her sex. Maybe she felt that if she could do it, so could anyone else. But not everyone is made of iron.

One bunch of women made of very strong stuff were the sewing machinists at the Ford plant in Dagenham who in 1968 went on strike and brought the mighty Ford Motor Company to a halt. Their fight for equal pay with their male co-workers was told in the film *Made in Dagenham*, released a few years ago. Incensed by being categorised as unskilled and paid accordingly, the women rose in revolt until Barbara Castle, the Employment Secretary in the Wilson Government, stepped in and began the process that led to the Equal Pay Act of 1970. During the strike, the women came under huge pressure to give in, not least from some of their husbands, many of whom also worked at the plant and whose own jobs were threatened by the possibility that Ford might close the plant for good and move their activities out of Britain. But the women held fast to their principles and won a historic victory.

I was sent to do portraits of some of the leading figures. When I arrived on one woman's doorstep, she looked me up and down with a surprised and disappointed expression.

'I'd been expecting Freddie Reed who does the royals,' she said. 'You're a woman. Do you think the pictures will come out?'

Which only goes to prove that, in the fight for equality, women's worst enemy is sometimes other women.

Chapter Thirteen

End of a Marriage

Tony always fled upstairs to his room. Little Catherine hid under her bed, too young to understand what was happening but frightened now of the father she loved. Jeanne, scared too but feisty, often stood her ground and shouted back.

As the years passed, Pierre gradually lost his battle with alcohol. Though there were still periods when he was relatively all right and able to work, the times when he was far from all right increased in frequency and lasted longer.

'Oh, Dad's in a funny mood,' was an expression which no longer did the job.

Luckily, the violence was largely directed at objects rather than people, though there were plenty of occasions when I thought he was going to hit me. Jeanne used to throw her little body in between us to protect me. It might have been better if he had in fact struck me because I think that would have ended the marriage and saved more long years of distress. But it never happened. Not quite.

So I wasn't a battered wife physically, but emotionally I was black and blue. The alcoholic rages were terrible. Exacerbated by the booze, the sadness inside him, the sadness that no amount of love from me and the kids seemed able to overcome, would suddenly erupt. He'd upturn a table covered in crockery, sending the china flying, the food and drink spilling over the carpet and the walls. Or he'd throw something through the window, the glass shattering into shards.

In the rages, all sorts of venom would spill out, like the lancing of a boil. Against his cold, domineering mother. Against the people he worked with and who didn't respect him or give him a chance. Against all the British. Against me, who'd forced him to come and live here against his will. Why was I so successful? he yelled, six inches from my face? Wasn't he just as good a photographer as I'd ever been? Better in fact? He'd been Picture Editor of *Le Figaro* at the age of twenty-six. Why hadn't he married a nice French girl, stayed in his beloved Paris, instead of being stuck in fucking Shortlands? He'd have been happy now. But no, he'd given everything up for me. Everything. The abuse poured out again and again. Always the same pain, the same questions. Most of which I couldn't answer.

Every time he suddenly flipped, I never knew what to do. Would it pass as before? Or might this be the time he finally crossed the line and hit either me or the kids, causing a serious injury or even worse? If I did nothing, might I regret it for the rest of my life?

God knows what the neighbours were saying behind the net curtains of Valley Road. My friend next door knew something of what was going on. She wasn't a gossip, but sometimes things slip out. Our house was detached but had people heard the noise as they walked past? Had they watched him on his way home from the station, unsteady on his feet? Or bumped into him and smelt his breath? But I couldn't bother too much about that. The welfare of the kids came first.

The evening finally came when I was forced to call the police. Pierre had thrown something else through the window, I can't remember what. Seeing policemen on my doorstep was almost as bad as seeing the bailiff there. They came in, made sure nobody had been hurt, gave Pierre a ticking-off and went away. In those days, such incidents were called 'domestics' and were not very high on the list of police priorities. There were no injuries, no threat to public order, not even any great 'disturbance of the peace' apart from the sound of breaking glass. Pierre had been inside his own home, which most people, certainly the male of the species, viewed as 'an Englishman's castle'. A Frenchman's too.

Despite all the things that were changing for the better in British culture, there were still huge numbers of men who believed they were the undisputed king of their castle and that 'the little lady' came a very definite second. Maybe those policemen were among them. Maybe they thought I was some difficult, shrewish wife who'd driven her husband to drink and the poor sod had finally stood up for himself. And, though it hadn't happened in his case, maybe they were even among those men who felt it was excusable to give a woman the occasional smack if she tried your patience. Who knows? Anyway, they were next to useless. Despite this, in the years to come, I'd have to call them again, more than once.

The next morning, Pierre remembered nothing of it. Not a thing. When I told him of course, the usual remorse set in. The protestations of regret, that he loved me and the children, that he'd try harder to get a grip on himself. It was heartbreaking to listen to, because I'd heard it all before. So many times. The words were almost meaningless now. In a way, the morning-after remorse was even harder to deal with than the night before. In the cold, sober light of day, I was seeing the real Pierre, the lucid, intelligent, loving Pierre. The man with an awful addiction that was ruining both his own life and our happiness as a family.

I felt pretty lost. Marje Proops did her best to help, but that was still about getting Pierre to Alcoholics Anonymous. No chance. No chance at all.

The other obvious source of support was my parents. But there were troubles in that household too. Len Spooner had retired around the time of our return to London. His last job had been as Editor of *Picture Post*, Britain's answer to *Life* magazine in the

States. But he'd not been terribly happy there and, as Fleet Street changed and a new generation of journalists and photographers grew up around him, he was glad to retire. I was pleased about that, thinking that his company around the house would be a real tonic for my mother, maybe even be the catalyst that would finally trigger some sort of recovery. Instead it only made the situation a whole lot worse.

Like many busy men who suddenly find themselves with nothing much to do, Dad looked around for something. Disastrously, he proceeded to interfere in the running of the home and to hijack many of the domestic tasks that had always been not just Mum's responsibility but her obsession. Without meaning to, he'd almost taken away her purpose in life.

She adored her grandchildren and they her. Compared to the scary Mègaby in France, Ada Spooner was saintly. Both she and my father smoked like chimneys, which was an odd habit for a woman obsessed with having a spotless house. To my annoyance, they also bought cigarettes for the kids. Nowadays that would be regarded as almost criminal, but then it was seen as a treat, albeit a naughty one. But sometimes the kids were a bit too much for my mother's fragile character, especially Tony, who could be a bit wild. The girls would tell me how Nana had followed them around the rooms of her house, nervously picking bits of fluff off the carpet. When Dad eventually decided they should move from south London to the countryside, I suspect that it was partly to shield Ada from the strain of the children.

They bought a house in Alfriston, a beautiful village in the South Downs near Eastbourne. But this too proved a serious mistake. Mum became even more isolated. She never settled in. While Dad grew his orchids and dahlias and did most of the chores, she sat there having little to occupy her beyond picking more fluff off the carpet inside a different four walls. Or maybe going to bed in the afternoon. The parallel with Pierre was painfully obvious. If only people would open up to those who love them, so much pain could be avoided.

Over the years, I was never clear how much my parents knew about the extent of Pierre's problem. Due to Mum's depressions, I tried to shield it from them as much as possible. No doubt the kids said things, especially as they got older. Maybe that was why my mother rarely came to our house. And despite the closeness between Dad and me, I didn't want to burden him any further. He had enough trouble on his plate. As for me, my worries about Pierre were made worse by my concerns about my mother. For all these years, I had not one but two sick people in my life, both of them seemingly incurable, beyond my help. The strain was considerable.

Despite Marje Proops' constant kindness, I could hardly go running into her office every bloody day. There were so many other staff who bent her ear, it's a wonder poor Marje ever had time to answer any readers' letters. But I really did need someone to lean on. I was still close to my old chum Fay from Wisbech, now married to our GP and living close by in Kent. As an adult, she had become a nurse and was used to comforting people in trouble, but if only her husband had tried harder to help Pierre. There was Madge too, another close friend from north London, but there was little either could do beyond lending an ear, hugely valuable though that was.

Pierre's work became more sporadic. Fleet Street was a very small world and even in this hard-drinking environment, he now had a reputation as a boozer, a boozer who, despite his talent, might be more bother than he was worth. Slowly but surely, the jobs fell away.

His brother Jean, working as a journalist with the World Health Organisation in Geneva, tried to give Pierre some work. A darkroom was set up in our garden shed, but the jobs were few and far between and soon the darkroom went back to being the home of spades and shovels.

By now, the family in France were all aware of the situation.

Mègaby didn't want to know. She didn't even want him to come and see her. So much for motherhood. In an attempt to help, Jean and his English wife, Renee, invited Pierre to stay with them for a while, even though Jean himself was struggling with cancer at that time. The two brothers had always been close and I hoped that Jean's affection and the strength of their childhood memories might somehow have an effect. Still I thought of my husband's drinking as something within his control and that a few sharp words from somebody he loved and respected might do something to pull Pierre, and all of us, back from the edge of the cliff. How naïve that was. After a while, Jean and Renee admitted defeat and Pierre came back home.

By the time the children were all teenagers, Pierre's relationships with his kids had taken a nosedive. He fought with Tony as much as he'd ever fought with his own mother. Even without Pierre's drinking that would have been the case; their characters were just too alike. The combination of a stroppy, wayward teenage boy and an alcoholic father was combustible. By now, both the girls were becoming partially estranged from their father and frightened for me. It was a hard thing to admit to myself, but I could see that, during the worst times, they even hated him. As they all grew older, they all began to distance themselves from the situation, staying out of the house as much as they could.

At this point, we no longer needed au pairs and I would find myself alone with Pierre more often. So many times I pleaded with him to stop drinking. He would sit there sullen and hopeless, staring at the floor or back at me, hardly bothering to reply. There were many tearful scenes.

By the mid-Seventies, it had been nearly fifteen years since the day of the bailiff, when I discovered my husband had a destructive addiction that had come to overshadow all our lives. For the first decade, I'd considered I'd had no choice but to hang on in there, largely for the sake of the children, but also because I couldn't bring myself to give up on the man I loved. But after fifteen years, I was getting worn down. There seemed to be no resolution, no answer to my prayers, just more of the same. As time passed, there were fewer and fewer 'good days' and eventually there were no days at all when Pierre wasn't drunk at some point.

Miraculously, however, he'd somehow managed to keep getting little bits of work and to lay off the booze during those hours he was actually behind a camera. He'd even landed a regular freelance slot at the *Daily Express*. It was a temporary reprieve. When they discovered he'd been fiddling his expenses to buy alcohol, he was fired – a trauma made worse by the fact that it was my cousin Carol's husband, John Lyth, who had to do the deed. It was the last press job he ever had. The end of his photographic career.

As his career had crashed and burned, my own had steadily climbed. Though other female photographers did contribute to British newspapers, I was still the only woman staff photographer on a Fleet Street tabloid. This simple fact had given me a certain profile and it was one that the *Daily Mirror* quite enjoyed bragging about. I was never any sort of real celebrity, but over the years my name would have become known, even vaguely, to the estimated 15 million people who read the paper every day.

This was hard for Pierre to swallow. Although alcohol was the major issue, there's no doubt that professional jealousy became another toxin in his decline. Over the years, I'd begun to beat myself up for everything that was wrong with my husband: if only I hadn't forced him to come to Britain, if only I hadn't been successful. If only, if only. It was hardly good for my own mental health.

One day, there was an old movie on TV called *A Star Is Born*. It featured Judy Garland as a young singer married to a famous actor who'd taken to drink. As her own star had risen, his had fallen and he'd ended up unemployed and unable to sort out his life. I was no star but as I watched it, I thought, 'This is us.' Or at least a suburban, south London version of the same story.

Back then, heaven help the woman who overtook her man in any way, got a better job than him, won more praise, earned more money. Now, in the 21st century, I hope this problem has at least diminished. Many young men seem less hung-up about such stuff, happy to be house-husbands while the wife is the main breadwinner. But I'd be surprised if it's not still something that rumbles underneath plenty of partnerships like a faultline.

As things got steadily worse Catherine, now in her late teens, urged me again and again to divorce her father. She could see how exhausted I was. By now, the world had moved on and the stigma of divorce had lessened greatly. Half the royal family had divorced already (and would go on doing so). But it had never really been that which had stopped me. I'd just wanted to do the best I could for all of us. But now, there was my daughter begging me to do the deed. If the kids now thought this was for the best, what was stopping me? A mixture, I suppose, of a stubborn refusal to accept defeat and my guilt at having taken him away from his beloved France. And the sight of that topaz engagement ring, which had once held so many hopes.

But my ability to cope was draining away. I read once that we all have a 'resilience tank' inside us. In tough times, we need to draw on it so that the level drops down. Then something good happens which raises it again. And so it constantly rises and falls depending on our joy or our misery. But if there is so much unhappiness that the 'tank' becomes nearly empty, we're in big trouble. In my case, it had been the love of the children and my work at the *Mirror* that had kept me going, but eventually even that wasn't enough. By the mid-Seventies, my resilience was almost gone.

After one particularly bad episode, I exiled him to our caravan in Deal, where he stayed for a few months over the summer. My sadness at the loss of him was balanced by an indescribable relief at not having him in the house. But the caravan wasn't habitable in the colder weather so, as winter came on, I had no choice but to take him back.

But in 1978, I finally did the deed and, after twenty-six years of marriage, Pierre and Doreen Vandeputte were divorced. I should have done it years before. In the long run, putting it off had helped nobody.

Absurdly, he carried on living in the house. He simply didn't have anywhere else to go. He was exiled to the small bedroom the au pairs had once occupied. A piece of paper from a judge doesn't stop you caring, doesn't switch off your heart. I bought him a small car to help him get around. Clearly, his photographic career was bust but he needed to try and find some kind of work. Not just to keep him afloat financially, but to give him a reason to get up in the morning. After all, he was only fifty-four. And he did go out and find a job. But when I heard what it was, I couldn't believe my ears. My ex-husband, the alcoholic, had got himself a job in an off-licence. As the modern expression goes, you couldn't make it up.

After a while, the craziness of the arrangement was obvious and I told him he really had to move out. We found him a small flat to rent in Chislehurst, just a couple of miles away, close enough to make it easy for him to see the kids. A nice enough flat, but not quite what he'd been used to in his life. It was hardly Valley Road. It was certainly a far cry from the house at Bois-Colombes or that grand, antique-filled apartment in the Rue de La Planche where he'd grown up. Mègaby, that difficult mother, died around this time. Pierre went alone to Paris for her funeral. Despite their tempestuous relationship, the removal of another fixture in his life couldn't have come at a worse time.

Tony, Jeanne and Catherine were young adults by now, taking the first important steps in their own lives. Exploring their possibilities and finding their different ways forward. They came and went as they chose and that was just fine with me. Every couple of weeks, they'd go over to Chislehurst and spend some time with their father, reporting back to me on his current state. Somehow, he seemed to be coping.

But though the house in Valley Road no longer echoed to the sound of rows and tears, Pierre was still very much present. A ghost at the feast. Whatever hell he'd put us all through, we still worried deeply about him and, in our different ways, loved him. That he still loved us too was never in doubt. Pierre was a Catholic and divorce for him was even harder than it had been for me. He'd said that he still regarded me as his wife and that he always would. And, till the day he died, I believe that he did.

At the end of the garden was an ancient air-raid shelter. Pierre had locked it up and fenced it off, claiming it was dangerous. But one day after he had gone, out of idle curiosity, I decided to break in. As my eyes adjusted to the darkness, I was amazed by what greeted me. From floor to ceiling, almost spilling out of the door, were hundreds and hundreds of empty vodka bottles. It was the saddest thing I ever saw.

At the moment he died in London, the girls and I were on a Greek island. Nobody could be precise about which day, let alone which hour or minute everything was over for him. So I don't know what we might have been doing just then. Maybe swimming in the warm sea, sunbathing on a lounger with the latest Jackie Collins, having a laugh in a taverna, three girls together, Jeanne, Catherine and me.

There was a closeness between me and my girls that had never existed between me and my own mother, much as we'd cared for each other. Partly that was the less formal times we now lived in, partly because the three of us just clicked as characters. I was proud of them and always loved being in their company.

I'd needed the break badly. Life at the *Daily Mirror* was as hectic as ever and by now I was over fifty. Thank God the cameras were getting ever lighter, but it was still the demanding job it had always been. And then we flew home.

Almost at once, I had to take off again on a quick assignment to the south of France. Just a couple of days away, I'd not even bothered to leave the girls the name of the hotel. In 1980, there were no mobiles or internet and it took the *Daily Mirror* a few hours to track me down. Catherine had called them. Pierre was dead.

They'd found him in his little flat in Chislehurst. A neighbour, concerned that she'd not seen him for a while, had called the police. They reckoned he'd been dead about ten days. A massive heart attack. He was fifty-six years old.

The *Mirror* flew me back to London at once. I sat on the plane, numbed by the shock and terribly sad, but I didn't cry. We all gathered at the house in Valley Road, trying to say the right things to one another.

At times like that, people seem to go onto automatic pilot. Arrangements had to be made and we made them. Calls were made to France, to his brothers and the wider family. Should we have finally sent him home to Paris, to some pretty churchyard near the grand apartment in the Rue de la Planche? But we didn't. We kept him near us. And so the funeral of Pierre Vandeputte-Manevy took place at St Joseph's Catholic Church in Bromley, after which he was buried in the nearby cemetery. I can't describe what happened that day, because I moved through it in a daze and then blotted it out.

After he'd moved out of Valley Road, he had often come back to it. Maybe that was a mistake, I don't know. All I knew was that somebody needed to keep an eye on him and if it wasn't me and our children, who on earth would? I'd give him a meal and we'd have a chat, mostly about the kids, of course. What were they up to, how was he getting on in the flat on his own, was he eating enough?

Sometimes, especially if one or more of the kids were there, it felt as if we were a proper family again. I could see Pierre felt that too. Every time he came over, it was painfully obvious that he wanted to stay and not go back alone to that little flat in Chislehurst. It was hard to watch him walk away down the garden path, then to close the door behind him.

God knows what he thought about sitting in that rented flat, no doubt with a drink in his hand. Because of that drink, he had lost everything. His wife, his home, his career, his reputation, his self-respect. He hadn't entirely lost his children. They visited him when they could, but they had their own lives by now. But everything else had gone.

How hard it must have been for him to sit there and think back to his early life. His student days at L'École des Beaux-Arts. Being admired for his talent and the huge promise he had shown. Working on *Le Figaro*. The beautiful Rita Hayworth autographing his shirt. His great shots of Churchill, The Beatles and scores of others. I have hundreds of Pierre's pictures to this day. He was a truly fine photographer. So at least some of Pierre's work remains. The booze couldn't destroy that, even if it did wreck everything else.

When somebody you've cared for dies, especially if the relationship hasn't been easy, your instinct is try to forget the rotten times, the disappointments and the pain. You attempt to focus on the good things, the happy memories, the joy that the person had brought you. And so, after those sad days of his death and funeral, so many images flicked through my head. In the Magnum office in Paris, being introduced to the handsome young Frenchman with the sexy accent. The dinners in the smoky bistros, the walks along the banks of the Seine. Asking me to marry him on the Pont Saint-Louis. Our first home, that snug little eyrie in the Rue de l'Estrapade with the windows looking out over the city. Such romantic, corny stuff. But all of it true. How on earth had it all gone so wrong?

Was it just because I'd made Pierre live in England? Or the xenophobia of Fleet Street? A wife being more successful than him? Did that really explain it all? Or was it maybe deeper than that? Never having had his real father in his life? That volatile relationship with his mother, who'd never shown him much affection? Even the things he'd seen in the war? I was no psychiatrist, so I would never know. Perhaps it was a psychiatrist who'd been needed all along.

All I knew for certain was that it was such a terrible waste. Until you've seen at close quarters what a devastating effect alcohol addiction has, you just can't understand. It is a terrible thing to witness. If it hadn't been for the booze, Pierre and I might still have been married to this day. When he was sober, he had been a wonderful man, warm and caring to me and his kids. I had so much for which to be grateful to him, not just for giving me those kids but for many other things. Just as my passion for photography had done, Pierre had opened my eyes to a wider, more exciting world.

What made his sudden, lonely death even harder was that, in recent months, he'd shown encouraging signs of drinking less. I began to wonder if the shock of the divorce had been his 'rock-bottom' point, that moment at which he'd turned the corner and finally faced the fact that he needed serious help. I'd had those hopes before of course and they'd turned to dust. But maybe, just maybe, there was light at the end of that long, long tunnel? I swore to myself that I'd never remarry him, but was there still, despite everything, some sort of future for the two of us? I'd never know the answer.

During this time, one very odd thing had happened. The morning that I'd had to fly to the south of France, I'd ordered a taxi to take me to the airport. It waited for me outside while I locked my cases, checked I had my passport, all those little, last-minute details. Suddenly, I heard Pierre's voice coming from outside the house. I wondered what he wanted. I really didn't have time to talk to him now or I might miss my plane. But when I went outside he wasn't there. Nowhere to be seen. Yet I'd heard him, clear as a bell. The voice that had once meant more to me than any other. How odd. But I had no time to worry about it then and jumped into the taxi.

On that morning, Pierre was in his flat a few miles away. Already dead.

Chapter Fourteen

Parting Shots

I was standing halfway up a stepladder on the Great Wall of China. The Duke of Edinburgh was right beside me, talking to a group of British exchange students.

'If you stay here much longer, you'll all be slitty-eyed,' he laughed.

'Ooh, you shouldn't have gone and said that,' I hissed, before I could stop myself.

'Don't you think?' he asked, looking up at the woman on the stepladder.

'No, I don't!'

And I was right, wasn't I? What a palaver ensued.

It was 1986. The historic royal tour of China. A fortnight in such an exotic place with the Queen might sound glamorous, but it wasn't. Before we left, we all had to be thoroughly vetted, checked for criminal records, all that stuff. At all times, a security pass would have to be worn around your neck which, it turned out, would get constantly entangled with the cameras. At one point, I almost hoped that my parking tickets might disqualify me from going at all.

For everyone involved, from the Queen downwards, these tours were a long hard slog. Vast stretches of boredom punctuated by frantic half-hours. The international press pack was huge. That's why I was standing on a stepladder. Determined that we Brits must get the best vantage points (well she was our Queen, after all), some bright spark had the idea of buying a job lot of fold-up steps. The theory was that since the Chinese tended to be on the short side, the ladders would lift us head and shoulders above them. We must have looked like a window cleaners' convention, but it worked a treat.

The stepladders, the photographers, the reporters and of course the royals dutifully trotted around the Forbidden City in Beijing, the Terracotta Warriors and every other interesting site. These were magnificent spectacles, but the royals didn't seem to be having a particularly good time. During the whole trip, I only managed to get one picture of the Queen smiling and that, no surprise, was at a horserace. On another day, she'd sat through a play put on by some children at a kindergarten with a face like thunder.

'For heaven's sake, Your Majesty, just one bloomin' smile,' I was muttering to myself.

I guess she was just tired. How many school plays had she sat through in her time? A hundred at least. A thousand probably. It was nearly forty years ago since I'd first photographed her at Clarence House when she was still Princess Elizabeth. She'd worked bloody hard since then, been through a lot. But then so had I. Back home, the Queen got lots of praise for her energy on this visit, she was sixty years old by now. But I was only two years younger and doing it weighed down with three cameras and that bloody stepladder.

If my face had rung a bell with Her Majesty, she never said so. Obviously, the royals got to recognise those photographers who specialised in covering their activities. Dear Freddie Reed had been held in great affection by them, and Kent Gavin, who succeeded him, certainly won their trust too. There's a great story about the Queen meeting a press photographer in Australia, at the time when her sister was still married to Lord Snowdon.

'So you're a photographer?' says the monarch, deducing this

from the cameras draped around his neck.

'Sure am, Ma'am.'

'That's a coincidence. My brother-in-law is a photographer.'

'A double coincidence, Ma'am,' replies the Aussie. 'My brother-in-law is a queen.'

Whether Her Majesty got the joke or not would be really interesting to know.

Being with the Queen and the Duke of Edinburgh on the Great Wall of China was certainly memorable. The Wall itself was an amazing sight, but what a shame to be seeing it covered with hordes of noisy, sweaty people, all chasing after the British monarch. I thought how wonderful it would be to stand here alone with my camera. To just drink it in for a while, then try and capture some of its spectacular beauty. It was on this trip I realised that while I'd lost none of my love of magical images, I was maybe beginning to lose my enthusiasm for the pressures of the newspaper life.

Apart from those breaks when I'd been raising the children in Paris, I'd now been a press photographer for nearly four decades. I'd had a good run, an amazing time. But that trip to China had been wearing. A bear garden. Some of the other press people had been less than charming. Even the royals hadn't been especially cooperative. I'd not taken any photographs I'd been really proud of, certainly no great 'picture'.

After Pierre died, I went on working at the *Daily Mirror* till I hit sixty in 1988. Nothing much changed in those years except that the 'golden age' of our fifteen-million readers had passed. Though we still remained a huge-selling newspaper, Rupert Murdoch's *The Sun* had gradually overtaken us. But this was the age of Thatcherism. In the Falklands War, after Britain had sunk the Argentinian ship *General Belgrano* with huge loss of life, *The Sun* had published its notorious headline 'Gotcha!'. Somehow, it seemed to embody the spirit of those times, which the Labour Party, and its loyal supporter the *Daily Mirror*, just weren't doing.

Yet it seemed more important than ever to be a voice for ordinary working-class folk. Through thick and thin (mostly thin), the *Daily Mirror* remained a Labour-supporting paper, even after the disastrous election of 1983, when it did catastrophically under the flag of the hard-left leader Michael Foot. He was succeeded by a young, charismatic firebrand called Neil Kinnock. But on the very day of Kinnock's crowning at the party conference, I took a photograph that the Tories would use to taunt him with for the rest of his leadership.

Kinnock and his wife, Glenys, went for a photo-call along Brighton Beach for the delectation of the usual press gang, including me. They strolled along the water's edge hand in hand, this attractive young couple, the last hope of the Labour Party. All went well till a sudden large wave caught them and Kinnock toppled over, flat on his back, his wife only just saving herself from the same fate. The photographers all clicked as fast as they could, but I'd gone one better. To get a good angle, I'd taken my shoes off and walked into the shallows. I was also using a Nikomat camera, which I'd switched over to automatic, meaning that I got many shots in rapid succession. Though other papers published similar images, I'd got easily the best ones and they were used around the world for several years to come. Sadly, as I say, mostly by the Tories.

The fact I'd used an automatic camera was deeply resented by some of my competitors on other papers. They thought it was somehow cheating. Many press photographers could be a bit reactionary and didn't always rush to embrace new technology. Oh well, more fool them. And if by some remote chance Lord Kinnock is reading this – sorry, Neil.

These were divisive years in Britain. Those not in thrall to Thatcher struggled to make their voices heard. One of the loudest yells of outrage was that of the Women's Peace Camp at Greenham Common. Thatcher's government had given permission for the USA to install Cruise nuclear missiles at this

RAF airbase in Berkshire. A protest, entirely of women, started slowly but grew into one of the largest ever seen in Britain. At its peak, 50,000 women joined hands to entirely encircle the base. They tried to break the fences and sat down in front of military vehicles. Hundreds were arrested and many imprisoned.

A city of tents and old caravans was gradually established around the perimeter of Greenham Common. Many women set up permanent residence, living there for weeks, months and, in some cases, even years. Conditions were quite rough, especially in the winter months. Squalid and miserable, it was very far from being any sort of picnic. When I was sent out to photograph them, I was appalled by the way they had chosen to live.

It has to be said that the British press, including those on the Left, was not very supportive of the Greenham Common protesters. The women had firmly excluded men from the camp, in order to emphasise that this was a movement of mothers, trying to protect the future of their children and grandchildren.

Most of the press responded by saying that the way to do so was to be back at home looking after them and not sitting in a cold tent in a muddy field. In other words, a woman's place was not to be making a fuss about a so-called 'political issue'. That should be left to the men. A woman's place was in the home. Despite the sexual revolution of the Sixties, despite Germaine Greer and Betty Friedan and the gigantic strides that feminism had made, that old attitude still lingered, like some disease you imagine has vanished but which suddenly flares up again. It was the same old mantra that my mother had tried to ram down my throat. The bailiff on the doorstep had obliged me to ignore her but I never kidded myself that I'd entirely succeeded in doing so.

So if I slightly disapproved of the Greenham Common women, it was probably because, deep down, I disapproved of myself. Now I look back on them with a bit more respect. After all, what were they doing that I hadn't already done, albeit in a very different way? Refusing to be stifled. Refusing to accept that their gender made their opinions any less valid.

Back in London, an explosive device of a different sort was about to be parked in the *Daily Mirror*. In 1984, we were bought by the media tycoon Robert Maxwell. With all his millions, he was supposed to be the saviour of the paper's flagging circulation. But the cure turned out to be worse than the ailment. In my view, he was a disaster for the paper. To this day, I blame some people on the board of the Mirror Group for taking the Maxwell 'shilling'.

On the surface, not much changed at minion level. Every day we still laboured to bring out a great paper for the British public to enjoy but, in the huge building on Holborn Circus, the atmosphere was different. Despite the inevitable squalls and storms, the petty jealousies and the big egos, we'd always been an essentially happy ship. Now it seemed overshadowed by this great black bat nesting up on the top floor.

I tried to keep out of Maxwell's way, but there were plenty who stuck their noses right up his very large arse. He really fancied himself with the ladies. To my utter bafflement, Marje Proops actually seemed to find him physically attractive. Personally, I'd rather have had it off with Genghis Khan.

It was impossible not to bump into him occasionally. I once left the office alongside him, right into the thick of a snowstorm. He was only wearing a suit and, even though it was Maxwell, the mother in me kicked in.

'You'll freeze to death!' I said. 'Don't you have a winter coat?'

'Oh, Miss Spooner,' he said, his eyes twinkling, giving me the once-over. 'I wish I had a woman like you to look after me.'

The Maxwell charm was being turned on full. It might work on Marje Proops and Anne Robinson but it bloody well didn't on me.

He was an incredibly vain man, his ego as big as the building itself. He was always finding an excuse to get his picture into the paper. Like me, though, not everybody was seduced. My dear friend Audrey Whiting, who'd introduced me to Pierre all those years ago in Paris, was one of those. She'd been at the paper even longer than me and was respected as one of the finest journalists in Britain, male or female. But she wasn't Maxwell's cup of tea at all, maybe because she was as tall as he was and could look him directly in the eye, rather than from below like most of his worshippers. She walked out in the early days of his reign, before he got around to firing her. The great John Pilger didn't move fast enough. He only lasted a year or so before being sacked, robbing the paper of one of its most respected writers. It wasn't a good period.

'What are you up to at the moment, Miss Spooner?' Maxwell once asked me in a corridor.

'I'm going out to the Seychelles to photograph a pop group, Mr Maxwell.'

'No you're not,' he replied, narrowing those big beetle eyebrows. 'You'll do it in the studio here.'

Bugger. I'd been looking forward to a bit of sun. Two days later I bumped into him again.

'What are you doing here?' the voice boomed. 'I thought you were going to the Seychelles.'

'I was, but you stopped it!' I barked back.

Maxwell glowered at me for a moment.

'Oh, all right then, you can go,' he said. 'But mind those expenses. I'm not made of money.'

It was a bit like working for the Emperor Nero. You never knew if you were going to be given a laurel wreath or thrown to the lions.

In his vanity, Maxwell liked to imagine he was adored, that he was really just 'one of the boys'. One year, he invited himself to the photographers' Christmas lunch. Nobody wanted him, but we could hardly tell him to sod off. It was grim. We couldn't let our hair down or get a bit tiddly, in case we said the wrong thing. It was like a wake, but without the laughs. A ghastly experience, still remembered by those who were there. Like the scene in *Macbeth*, where Banquo's ghost turns up at the dinner table.

If only Robert Maxwell had really been a ghost, a figment of our imagination. After his mysterious drowning off the Canary Islands in 1991, it turned out he'd been right when he'd told me he wasn't made of money. His media empire collapsed with debts of hundreds of millions. It was then revealed that he'd tried to hold things together by massive, illegal borrowing from the pension funds of the Mirror Group. I was retired by then and, thank God, my pension was safe. The government stepped in and helped to some extent but many people, especially in the printing unions, ended up with less than half the money they were entitled to.

All kinds of wild conspiracy theories went around about whether the great black bat was really dead or not. Was the drowning staged to escape the financial disaster about to hit him? Is his body really inside the coffin buried on the Mount of Olives in Jerusalem or is it just a pile of heavy stones? Is he living quietly in some remote valley in Switzerland or in a rainforest in Brazil, the hair now snow-white, the face surgically altered? Hopefully not. I'm not a malevolent woman, but I like to think that the fish of the Atlantic Ocean polished him off long ago.

As the troubled Eighties rolled on and the age of sixty loomed at me through the mists, I began to stop fearing the approach of retirement. And finally the big day came.

A great fuss was made, which was a bit embarrassing but also very touching. Anne Robinson wrote a kind farewell article about me, which was sweet of her. Telegrams and telexes (remember those?) came in from other Fleet Street papers. The messages were all so generous, not just about my work but about me as a person, and that meant just as much. Messages came too from *Mirror* colleagues working abroad. Kent Gavin sent one from Australia, where he claimed to be jogging along Bondi Beach with Princess Diana. Jammy bugger. Another telegram listed all the disasters they thought would befall the photographers' room in my absence. Who would get the coffees? Who would clean up the studio after Kent Gavin? Who would stop Monte Fresco farting?

The paper threw not one but two big parties. I'd been there so long that I knew too many people for just one 'do'. There was a swanky dinner hosted by the *Mirror* bigwigs at the Drury Lane Hotel, then, a couple of weeks later, an equally posh lunch for all my chums at The Ivy, London's most fashionable restaurant. Everybody came to one or the other: Marje Proops, Anne Robinson and most of my 'boys', past and present. I had to stand and make a speech. I tried to make it funny, but it was hard not to be a bit emotional. They gave me a huge framed photograph featuring every single face I worked with. I treasure it to this day. It sounds corny, but I really felt that it was me who should be thanking them.

For the preceding twenty-six years, the *Daily Mirror* had been the focus of my life, not forgetting that first short period in the late Forties when they'd given me my first chance and I'd repaid it by swanning off to America. But I hoped I'd made up for the disloyalty I'd shown back then. I'd never wanted to work anywhere else. Unlike a lot of press people, I'd not moved from paper to paper in search of more money or status. I'd long since realised that, for me, the *Mirror* was home.

As I stood making my speech in The Ivy, looking out onto the sea of familiar faces, it was hard to believe I'd not be seeing them on Monday morning as usual. A few had become like the brothers and sisters I'd never had. In the stressful times, I'd leant on them and, in theirs, they'd leant on me. Life without them was going to be very strange.

The spectre of that Monday morning was already growing in my mind. How weird not to be going from Shortlands Station into Holborn Viaduct, walking past the statue of Prince Albert in the centre of Holborn Circus and into that buzzing, extraordinary place. What in God's name was I going to do? Sit out in the garden and watch the bees pollinating the flowers? Would I even be able to breathe outside the grubby air of the newsroom?

All the tributes were wonderful, but I had to face the fact that the party was over. And British Rail decided to pay me a tribute too. On the very day I retired, they shut down Holborn Viaduct Station for good. If Doreen Spooner no longer needed it, what was the point of keeping it open?

'Let's have a little jaunt across the Channel,' one of the kids said.

'A nice trip to Boulogne,' said another. 'Stay overnight in that hotel we used to go to with Dad?'

'What do you think, Mum?'

'If you like, love,' I replied.

I wasn't that bothered. After all the fuss, I'd gone a bit flat. Post-career depression. Maybe a bit of sea air would do me good.

We arrived at the hotel in Wimereux, just along the coast from Boulogne. It was a place full of memories. Memories of Pierre and those times when the family was still in one piece. There were still few days when I didn't think of him at some point. And all three of our children looked so like him that his face was always with me.

We arrived in the early evening and I was tired from the journey. I said I might just skip dinner and go to bed. Jeanne and Catherine looked horrified.

'You can't do that'

'Why ever not?' I replied.

'Oh come on, Mum. We're on holiday.'

'Oh, all right then. But I'm not getting all dolled-up.'

'But you must. You really must.'

'For heaven's sake, is the Queen coming?' I asked.

No she wasn't, but everybody else had. When we walked into the lounge, I got the shock of my life. About thirty people were there, each one of them holding up a copy of the *Daily Mirror* to hide their faces. They lowered them to reveal a great gang of my extended family and oldest friends, including Pierre's brother Jean and his wife, Rene, my Dad's brother, Uncle Frank, and my little grandson, Thomas. I was cheered to the rafters. It was an unforgettable night. How kind people can be. That night, I knew I was loved and there's nothing to compare with that. Nothing at all.

But three people had been missing from that party. People who should have been there and without whom there would have been no career to celebrate. Pierre of course because, despite the jealousy that crept in later, he'd always respected my work and encouraged me to push myself further. He should have been by my side that night. If it hadn't been for the demon drink, he would have been.

The other two absentees were Len and Ada Spooner, Dad and Mum. Soon after Pierre died, I'd persuaded them to end their exile in Alfriston and return to a small flat in Beckenham, where I thought they might be happier and where I could keep a closer eye on them. But it was to be no magic wand. Still Mum complained to me that Dad hardly talked to her, at least not about things that mattered. That child she had lost all those years ago. That empty cradle beside her hospital bed, which had so devastated her that she had never been the same again. Back then, people were taught to pull themselves together and get on with life. There was no post-trauma counselling on tap. The men of my Dad's generation, however loving he might have been, just weren't geared to deal with such stuff. A tight hug and a strong cup of tea were probably the best he managed.

So Mum's illness was never to be resolved. One day she'd be functioning, the next she'd be back in bed. Right at the end of her life in 1983, she wouldn't get up for five days. Poor Dad was beside himself. An old man by now, he was in despair and just couldn't cope. I called the local hospital, who came and took her into their old people's unit. She was furious with me. The next day was Mother's Day and on that day she passed away. I felt her sudden end had been my fault, but I'd not known what else to do. She'd never approved of my having a career but I know she'd grown proud of me nevertheless. It must have been hard for her to see me buzzing around the world when she'd had her wings clipped so cruelly in her early life. Despite her illness, Mum did her best with the cards that had been dealt her. What more can any of us do?

After my mother died, Dad stayed in his flat for a while, then came to live with me in Valley Road. Despite Mum's problems, they had loved each other to the end and he missed her terribly. But what he needed now was a life free from stress and anxiety and I tried to make sure he had it. He'd been one of the best-loved figures in Fleet Street, respected and liked by everyone. Quite a feat in the often cut-throat world of newspapers. The best photographers of the 20th century had been his friends: Henri Cartier-Bresson, Robert Capa, Karl Gullers and many others. He'd certainly been an amazing friend to his only child. Without his encouragement and support, I'd never have made it. He never tried to hold me back or tie me down. He understood the damage which had been done to Mum as a girl and wasn't going to let that mistake be repeated. And so he let me fly. He died in 1985 and it was like losing a limb.

In 1988, I was sixty years old. My husband was long dead, my parents now gone too. My three children still came and went from the house in Valley Road, though Jeanne and Tony were both married now, so I saw less of them. I'd just retired from a job I'd loved. That great party the kids had organised in France seemed like a line being drawn under my life as I'd known it till now. As I looked out from the ferry at the White Cliffs of Dover rising out of the sea, I wondered what the hell I was going to do now.

Chapter Fifteen

Camera Granny

'I need Doreen Spooner. That's who I bleedin' need,' yelled the Picture Editor.

'She's retired, boss,' replied somebody. 'Or did nobody tell you?'

'This job is dead right for her. Dead right. Where is she?'

'Growing roses probably. Or tanning her tits on the Riviera.'

'Well find out where she is. Get her on the fucking phone.'

After making such a big fuss, after all the parties and the speeches, the *Daily Mirror* seemed oddly reluctant to let me go. After I officially retired, they still called me up to do the odd jobs here and there. I hesitated at first. I didn't really need the money, but it seemed daft to turn down a few hundred quid for a day's work. Especially if a grandchild needed a sub or there was a sale in my favourite dress shop. I suppose it made the wrench of retiring a bit easier, gradually weaning yourself off it instead of going cold turkey. As I'd feared, that first Monday when I didn't do the usual walk to Shortlands station had been a challenge. The rainy day had stretched out ahead of me like an endless, deserted road.

But after a while, I let these jobs trickle away. Either I was retired or I wasn't. It had been a great career and I was grateful for almost every minute of it. Grateful enough to feel that I should try and give something back to the profession.

Freddie Reed, the royal photographer, suggested I take his place on the board of the press photography section of the National Council for the Training of Journalists. For several years, I went up to Sheffield, gave talks and helped compile and judge the examination papers of eager young folk who wanted to be newspaper photographers. It was very satisfying to feel you were helping kids on their way, just as I'd been helped in my own time. Guiding them past the pitfalls, over the hurdles and opening their eyes to the endless possibilities of the career they'd chosen. The students were still overwhelmingly male but there were a few girls. Not long ago, one came up to me at some event and flung her arms around my neck.

'Oh, Doreen. We girls couldn't have done it without you!' she gushed. But it was sweet and I was touched.

As you'll have gathered from these pages, I never really saw myself as much of a feminist. I certainly had no political agenda. But I suppose I do like to think of myself as a trailblazer, somebody who wasn't going to let something as trivial as my gender stop me from doing what I wanted to do and express those talents that had somehow blossomed inside me.

A few years before I retired, I'd bought a small house for weekends in Polegate near Eastbourne. My old school friend Madge lived there and I knew the area from the time my parents had lived at nearby Alfriston. It's a lovely location; the South Downs on one side, Beachy Head and the sea on the other. Pretty villages, country pubs, old manor houses hidden in the folds of the hills. Such fresh, clean air. A whole different world from London.

'Your grass is a bit of a disgrace,' said my next-door neighbour one day.

'I'm only here at weekends,' I replied, 'and it's a shame to spend half the time mowing the lawn.'

'I could look after it for you, if you like,' he said. 'No trouble at all.'

Maybe he felt it was letting down the look of the avenue and might affect property values. So I accepted the offer. His name was John Davey. He seemed a pleasant chap, but even after he started being my unpaid gardener, I didn't get to know him or his wife particularly well.

But after I retired, I took the big decision to move to Polegate permanently. My parents were gone and the children didn't really need me close by. I worried in case I was too much of a Londoner to settle in such a quiet place. After all, my mother had been miserable in the country, but I wasn't my mother so I decided to take the risk. The weekend house in Spurway Park was too small to live in all the time, so I sold it and bought a bigger bungalow with a glorious garden in the same avenue. It was a new life and I loved it.

When Pierre died, I was just over fifty. Not quite over the hill yet. Under the influence of all the fashion photography I'd done, I'd developed a love of clothes and always tried to dress well and look as good as I could. I still wasn't Lana Turner, but there was the occasional flattering comment. Once I'd mourned Pierre for a time, I gradually began to accept the occasional invitation. It was hard at first because there had never been any man in my life other than my husband, but after dipping my toe in the water it became a little easier and it did me good. But I certainly wasn't desperate to find a bloke for a fling, let alone a serious relationship.

Once I'd gone to Polegate full-time, I cut my own front lawn, but my old neighbour John still popped in from around the corner. By now, his poor wife had died of cancer and we were now two people living on their own. As the years passed, he and I spent more and more time together. It was a very slow thing, very different from those breakneck infatuations of youth, but to my amazement, I realised that, at the age of seventy years old, I had fallen in love again and that it was mutual.

After a while, it seemed absurd that we lived in separate houses so, quietly and without any fanfare, John sold his own and moved in with me. I was firm about not wanting to marry again, so we became two old-age pensioners living 'in sin'. My mother would have disapproved and I suspect a few of the neighbours did too. After all, it was a highly respectable road. Even my friend Madge was a bit sniffy about it, though I reckon she was just jealous. There wasn't a lot of male totty around these parts and I'd bagged the best of them.

John Davey and I were given ten years together and, in some ways, they were the best ten years of my life. After all the stresses of my marriage to Pierre and the lifelong anxiety about my mother, I was in a safe haven. John brought me peace. I hadn't realised how much I'd needed that until, so unexpectedly, I found it.

He was such good company. Always full of fun and high spirits. Like Pierre, he drank quite heavily, a fact which worried me at first, but I never once saw him drunk. Maybe that was because he was at ease with himself, a man who, as the saying goes, 'fitted his skin'. He was an old-school ex-army type who'd been a big cheese in the Rank Organisation, responsible for its finances nationwide. He'd known lots of film stars, so he wasn't the least impressed by my chattering about famous faces I'd photographed. In fact, as time went on, I realised that I spoke less and less about Doreen Spooner, the photographer. It was almost as if she was somebody else altogether, only vaguely related to me. Sometimes, on a day when I had nothing planned except a stroll around the shops in Eastbourne, I'd imagine what might be happening in the *Mirror*. What was today's big story? Where might Kent Gavin be going that morning? If I concentrated, I could almost smell the newsroom and felt a slight pang of yearning.

But those thoughts didn't intrude too often. John and I led a quiet life 'in sin' among our friends in Polegate, spiced up with little trips abroad. I'd never been to Belgium from where the Vandeputtes had come, so John took me there and also to Germany, where his late wife's family lived. I had been nervous about how they'd react to me, but they were wonderful and happy that John had found someone new to share his life with. Mostly though, we just did what people do at the end of long careers – rested on our laurels, took things a bit easier, enjoyed the huge stroke of good fortune of having found each other and having our lives transformed by it.

All our children came to visit, my three and John's two daughters from his first marriage, with whom I got along fine. Nobody pretended to be anyone else's new 'mother' or 'father'. We were both well past that sort of nonsense and so were the 'children'. My kids were all in their forties by now. Throughout my life, I'd spent so much time worrying about how they'd turn out. They'd not had it easy. Growing up in a house overshadowed by an alcoholic father of whom they'd sometimes been afraid and a mother who was absent more than she should have been.

Jeanne and Catherine were, and still are, the best daughters a mother could wish for. Though chalk and cheese in some ways, they looked very alike and both were smart, creative and intelligent women. Both drifted into the rag trade and today they work side by side in an international fashion house. Jeanne married Gordon and Catherine married Chris, providing me with two lovely, supportive sons-in-law. Jeanne gave birth to Millie who, in her turn, has now provided me with a great-granddaughter. Millie is a gifted amateur photographer who specialises in shooting babies, so my original passion is now being realised through her.

So my two girls have done OK. It pleases me so much when they insist that, despite the tragedy of their father, their childhood was not an unhappy one. They concentrate on the good memories they have of him. The birthdays and the Christmases, the holidays at the caravan in Deal and the summers at Mègaby's in the country. All those moments when he was gentle and caring, when there was no booze in his bloodstream and he could be the person he really was. Both claim that the main legacy of the bad times is that, as adults, they always avoid arguments and run away from confrontation of any kind. But Jeanne and Catherine knew that they were loved by both their parents and there can be no more important thing for any child to feel. They are content in their lives and the knowledge of that makes me content in mine.

My son, Tony, was another matter. His head teacher at Alleyn's school in Dulwich said Tony was one of the cleverest pupils he'd ever taught, before expelling him for breaking another boy's nose. Tony verged on genius, but he had a wild, irrational streak that blighted his whole life.

If Pierre's addiction had been to alcohol, Tony's was to money. He got a kick out of making it and an even bigger kick out of spending it. He saw himself as a brilliant entrepreneur, but he wasn't. He'd have amazing ideas but somehow couldn't follow them through. At one time, he owned the rights to the newly introduced breathalyser machine, which could have made him a fortune, but instead sold them to make a quick killing. He liked all the flashy things money could buy. Eventually, he took a very wrong path and ended up in prison in America. It wasn't the last time he'd be behind bars. I'd always tried to make sure all my kids had a firm grounding in what was right and wrong, but somewhere along the way Tony had lost his moral compass. I believe that, of all people, my dear Dad bore some responsibility for this. Tony was the son he'd never had and my father spoiled him rotten, which led Tony to believe that he had some sort of right to the better things in life.

He had the charm of the devil, was married four times and had several more relationships. I used to collect daughters-in-law, legal or not, the way other people collect porcelain. There are no less than four grandchildren, one in America, who I never see and that is a hard thing to bear. But, by his first marriage, Tony gave me a grandson of whom I'm very proud. Thomas Vandeputte is now a professional photographer and carries the flame into the new century. He listens patiently to his old granny's advice and her tales of Fleet Street with what appears to be genuine interest. He's also blessed me with two more gorgeous great-granddaughters.

In 2015, Tony died suddenly at the age of only sixty. For some years, he'd lived in Gran Canaria with his partner. We spoke on the phone, but I rarely saw him. I made the hard decision not to go to the funeral because I'm an old girl now and I just didn't feel I could do it. But I was glad to hear how many people had gone to mourn him and how much he had been respected and even admired by his friends. It is an awful shock for any mother when her child dies before her. It is not how life is meant to be. On the day, Jeanne and her husband were in Gran Canaria to say goodbye to him; in London, Catherine and I went out for lunch and raised a glass to our wild son and brother. I'd so often feared what negative impact their childhood might have on my kids. But it was only in Tony that those fears were realised. I never achieved my dream of having six children and now I have only two left. And that is a very hard thing.

Some time before Tony passed away, there had been another death. My partner, John, had become ill with cancer and I finally lost him in 2013. Of the deaths I had faced in my life, of Pierre, my parents and even of my own son, all of whom I loved, that of John was perhaps the hardest to bear. We only had that one decade together, but they say it's the quality of life that matters, not the quantity. If so, then those ten years were threaded with gold.

John had given so much to me. At our age, it was hardly the great sweeping romance, violins playing, that it might have been when we were young. Polegate wasn't Paris, Spurway Park wasn't that little flat in the Rue de L'Estrapade and our back garden wasn't the banks of the Seine. But in that garden, I found companionship and a deep contentment. There was no greater pleasure than to sit under the pergola on a summer evening with a bottle of wine and look out over the flowers and shrubs we'd planted together. In that garden, I'd found my soulmate. Pretty late, but better late than never. The loss of him was dreadful.

It's 2016. I'll be eighty-nine years old at my next birthday. As I once stroppily predicted in the newsroom of the *Daily Mirror*, 'Camera Girl' has indeed become 'Camera Granny'. Great-granny in fact, something that amazes and thrills me. I've had a long life and I'm not done yet.

These days I live in a pretty flat near Surbiton on the outskirts of greater London. Catherine and Jeanne live close by. It's not big but it's fine for one and it's good to know somebody will come running if I pull a cord. What happened to poor Pierre will not happen to me.

In this block of flats, people know me as Doreen Vandeputte (I never saw any point in dispensing with my married name). For the last twenty years, Doreen Spooner has more or less ceased to exist. She has remained in the dark, hidden inside the pages of an endless number of photo albums kept in Catherine's attic or deep in the archives of the *Daily Mirror*, Getty Images or Magnum Photos. I confidently expected that she would remain there forever, but a few years back, an enterprising ball-of-fire called Dede Millar put together an exhibition in London in aid of breast cancer research. Called *She-Bop-A-Lula*, it showcased portraits of female singers photographed by the best female photographers from around the world. I was honoured to be included with my shots of Lulu, Sandie Shaw and Sade. Well into my ninth decade, it was a big thrill to stand in a swanky gallery and see those old photographs, in big newly minted prints, staring down at me. Doreen Spooner had come briefly back into the daylight, but I didn't imagine it would last for long.

But I reckoned without Dede Millar and my daughters. They'd put their heads together and hatched a plan. Far from having messed up their lives, it turns out both my girls are quite proud of having Doreen Spooner for a mother. Dede, Jeanne and Catherine thought that my story, both as a photographer and as a woman, reflected many of the things that the female of the species still has to deal with today. Trying to balance a career with being a wife and mother. Being a working woman in a world which, despite the odd president and prime minister, is still dominated by men. Coping with the possibility of achieving more than the man in your life. The girls believe there are still plenty of Doreen Spooners out there, although now they may have purple hair, tattoos and piercings and are almost certainly not called Doreen. And that the various pictures of my experiences might resonate with women in this new, scary century. I hope so.

Writing this book has been an odd experience: nostalgic, sentimental, often fun and sometimes very difficult. But Doreen Spooner has come out of the darkness and that has been a valuable thing. I don't intend to let her slip out of my reach again.

I rarely pick up a camera now. My eyesight is badly affected by macular degeneration, which is a bugger and no mistake. An ironic fate for someone whose life revolved around her vision. But I guess that, at nearly ninety, you've got to expect a few bits to fall off. So I guess I've taken all my pictures, captured my final images of this wonderful, complex world. Now I must leave it to my grandson, Thomas, and all the other hot young photographers to go on recording how humanity evolves in the years to come.

Of course, there's never been a time in which photography was so much at the centre of people's lives. These days, everyone's a photographer. With smartphone technology, half the human race is taking fifty pictures a day, seven days a week. It's no longer just a hobby or even an art form, it's an addiction.

I suppose the essence of the change is that, in my day, we only wanted to capture images that we felt had some value or significance – people we loved or admired, events that were memorable, unusual or in some way fascinating. In the digital age, that criterion has largely vanished. Now people photograph what they're having for breakfast, their baby's first poo or a pimple on the end of their nose. Then they upload it onto Facebook and invite all their friends to share the wonder of it. Extraordinary. It seems to me that if what you photograph is of no value, then the business of photography is somehow diminished. But then, I'm just an old girl from a different age.

When photography was invented in the 19th century, it was regarded as a miracle, a sort of magic, but the narrow province of a few dazzling pioneers. In the 20th century, it slowly became something everyone could do, yet still we venerated photographic geniuses such as Henri Cartier-Bresson, Robert Capa, Margaret Bourke-White, Don McCullin, Jane Bown and many others who recorded contemporary life in all its splendour and ugliness, its achievements and its follies. Even for those of us in the commercial hurly-burly of Fleet Street, always working against the bloody clock, we still saw our job as being something akin to an art. It mattered to us that whatever talent we possessed was apparent in the work we produced. When we had a shouting-match with the Picture Editor over which of our shots should be used, that was the reason. Even if it was just Jean Shrimpton walking along a catwalk, a poodle jumping through a hoop or a beautiful baby contest, the quality of it was important. For me, it's a little sad to see a world awash with pictures, but so few of them really worth taking.

In the early 21st century, Fleet Street remains as a geographical location. Parallel with the river, it still runs from the Law Courts up towards the dome of St Paul's Cathedral, the stonework of both now bright and shining in the sun, long since scrubbed clean of the soot and grime in which they were coated when I first went there almost seventy years ago. But 'Fleet Street', the almost mythical heart of Britain's newspaper industry is long gone. Driven out by the need to cut costs and by changing methods of production, the great glass palaces of the press closed their doors one by one and went elsewhere.

The old *Mirror* building at Holborn Circus has long gone, the site now occupied by the headquarters of a supermarket chain.

Where Marje Proops once sat answering readers' letters, where Maxwell once prowled the corridors, where Anne Robinson and Alastair Campbell once crafted their dazzling articles, executives now debate the pros and cons of opening a new branch in Scunthorpe. Today, the *Daily Mirror* offices are twenty-two floors above the pavement in that soaring tower at Canary Wharf. There is no smoking in the newsroom anymore; it is against the law, a fact that most of the blokes I once worked with would find totally incomprehensible. Now, every man will be safely deodorised, gelled and probably moisturised too. It's a safe bet that 'effing and blinding' is frowned upon in case anyone is offended and might need counselling. In the basement of the soaring tower are no huge printing presses waiting to thunder into life every night. The printing is now done far away. The world must move on and there can be no looking back. Except for us oldies, no longer in the thick of it.

Today in Fleet Street, the atmosphere is very different. With the glass palaces all gone, it seems a boring thoroughfare to those of us who once lived our lives there. The lawyers are still around, the boys and girls from The Temple and Lincoln's Inn, but they were always a very different tribe to the newspaper people. We were all much more fun. But now it's a street of Starbucks and Costa Coffee, of endless mobile phone stores and of shops selling shirts and ties for sharp-suited businessmen who work in IT or financial services.

But for me there are ghosts everywhere. It was here I came to visit my Dad at the *Daily Herald* when I was still in pigtails and saw the wonderful chaos of a newspaper for the very first time. Here still stands the building that was once the Bolt Court photographic school, along with the church of St Bride's, beautiful as ever, where Pierre and I were married more than sixty years ago.

Nowadays, some of us creak nearly as much as the old boards beneath our feet. We're all getting a bit wobblier, a bit frailer. We also get fewer and that is a painful thing. But for a few cheery hours we bring those we've lost roaring back to life, we salute their talents and tell stories about them, some of them even true. We tell stories about ourselves too and, in doing so, bring ourselves back to life, at least as we used to be. We remember dear Marje, cigarette holder permanently glued to her lips, swanning off for lunch at Claridge's in the back of her chauffeur-driven limo. We remember Robert Maxwell and shudder. We remember Prince Philip coming into the photographers' room demanding to know who shot the girly pictures. I remind Kent Gavin that I climbed to the top of Crazy Horse Mountain when he only managed halfway. I describe for the umpteenth time, standing in the door of that ladies' loo, trying to get 'those two tarts', Christine and Mandy.

But most of all we simply remember the thrill of being part of an extraordinary phenomenon called Fleet Street. Not always kind, not always admirable, but always exciting, challenging and, on the whole, with its heart in the right place. For any junior, doing their apprenticeship on some dull provincial paper, it shimmered like Camelot on the distant horizon. So much of its magic was in the camaraderie you might find there. And when we all meet up again, it's as if it was just five minutes ago.

After a few hours, you suddenly realise that you're feeling twenty years younger, such is the power of those memories. It's only when you try to stand up that you remember the passing of the years. We decant ourselves out into Fleet Street, looking for a taxi or bus that's going to take us back to wherever we all live now. We hardly need to look where we're going because we know every inch of this street, every twist and turn of it. Hands are clasped and shaken, backs are slapped and I am hugged by more men in five minutes than I will be for the rest of my days. We make jokes about seeing each other this time next year, if the Grim Reaper doesn't get us first, praying in our hearts that this is just a joke. Then we dissolve into the darkness of the late December afternoon.

In the taxi, I get a nosey driver.

'Christmas lunch, love?'

'Yes. Old colleagues. Annual knees-up.'

'What did you all do then?'

'Photographers. On the *Daily Mirror.*'

'Really? I had Marje Proops in the cab once,' he says. 'Did you know her? '

'Oh, yes.'

Quite a girl, old Marje.'

'She sure was.'

'So who have you photographed in your time then, love?'

I name-drop all the way around the Aldwych and across Waterloo Bridge. I start with Albert Einstein and George Bernard Shaw and finish with Blondie and Spandau Ballet. I even dredge up Christine and Mandy. He is suitably impressed.

'But weren't you the only woman in that crowd back there?' he asks.

'Yes.'

'Why was that then?'

'I really don't know,' I reply. And that's the truth. I still don't really have the answer to that one.

'Well, love,' he laughs as the taxi pulls into Waterloo Station. 'Pardon me, but you must have had balls.'

I walk into the station concourse, heaving with people, lots of them flushed from their own festive lunches. I find my train and return to Surbiton and my small flat. And go back to being a little old lady.

Acknowledgements

Firstly, I must thank Dede Millar who first ordered me to write a book. Without her energy, commitment and bullying, it would never have happened. My daughters Jeanne and Catherine have been a constant encouragement at every stage, but I must single out Cathy who, in the midst of a hectic life, has devoted an extraordinary amount of time to looking after my photographic archive and to digging out the pictures for this book.

I'm both delighted and touched that 'Camera Girl' is being published by my old 'gang'. I greatly appreciate the enthusiasm and expertise of everyone at Trinity Mirror, especially my editor Jo Sollis, sub-editor Robin Jarossi, art director Julie Adams, publishing director Paula Scott and head of syndication Fergus McKenna. It's good to know that, in the twenty-first century, the paper is in such talented hands.

Finally, my enormous gratitude goes to the writer Alan Clark who, over the past year, has gently extracted my memories with skill, determination and endless cups of strong tea. We've had a few wistful moments but mostly lots of fun.

Doreen Spooner

Also by Mirror Books

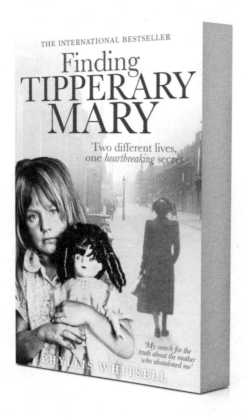

THE SUNDAY TIMES BESTSELLER
FINDING TIPPERARY MARY

The astonishing real story of a daughter's search for her own past
and the desperate mother who gave her up for adoption.

Phyllis Whitsell began looking for her birth mother as a young
woman and although it was many years before she finally met her,
their lives had crossed on the journey without their knowledge.
When they both eventually sat together in the same room,
the circumstances were extraordinary, moving and
ultimately life-changing.

This is a daughter's personal account of the remarkable
relationship that grew from abandonment into love,
understanding and selfless care.

Also by Mirror Books

Eating the Elephant

A shocking but inspiring true story that tackles the dark, modern crisis of internet pornography in a frank and groundbreaking way.

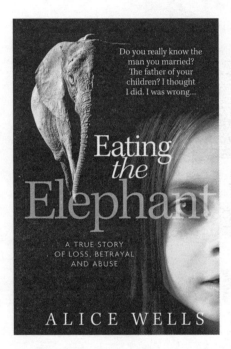

Alice, a dedicated doctor and mother of two children, bravely tells the story of her marriage to a man hiding a terrible secret – one into which he has drawn their 4-year-old daughter, Grace. As the shocking truth about their family life unfolds at a heartstopping pace, Alice struggles to learn how to survive the impact and piece together her shattered world.

The devastation of what she is forced to face when her life is hit by catastrophic pain, and the horror of wondering if she overlooked the signs, is laid bare in a moving and honest way that will stay with you for a long time to come.

How do you eat an elephant?
One piece at a time

"Before you venture into the pages that follow I feel compelled to issue a health warning. I urge you to take reasonable protective steps in order that you are equipped to enter what is, in emotional terms, a hard-hat area..."

Alice Wells* is a UK doctor. She has two children. This is her first book. *pseudonym*

Also by Mirror Books

'It felt like the right time to tell my own story, in my own words...'

After years of remaining silent, Anne Darwin finally reveals the truth
behind the crime that tore her family apart

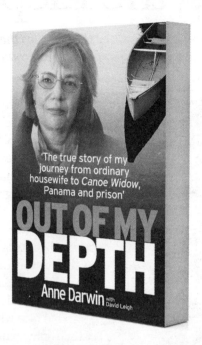

OUT OF MY DEPTH

When Anne Darwin told the world – and her family – that her husband,
John, had disappeared while canoeing in the North Sea, her life changed
forever. She had just lied to the police, the press, their friends, insurance
companies and her own sons. While her husband hid next door, Anne claimed
the life insurance, endured police questioning, accepted consolations – then left
with him to start a new life in Panama. For the first time, Anne opens up about
an extraordinary chain of events: her decision to take part in her husband's
hare-brained scheme; her life and marriage; her harrowing time behind bars
and the runaway train of deceit and guilt that followed their plan to defraud
insurance companies with the aid of a canoe.

*Anne's fee for this book goes directly to the RSPCA and the RNLI

See mirror collection.co.uk to order - or call 0845 143 0001
Also available on Kindle and in the iBook store